The Eberly Library
Waynesburg University

Waynesburg, Pennsylvania

• Advance Praise •

"Ray Comfort delivers yet another insightful and soul-stirring masterpiece for the ages. He does more than shed light on one of history's most notable geniuses—he daringly explores the infinite Mind that fashioned the finite one, and leaves his readers at the threshold of awe and wonder."

—**Emeal Zwayne, cohost of *The Comfort Zone***

"Einstein once said, "Anyone who doesn't take truth seriously in small matters cannot be trusted in large ones either." Ray Comfort has done it again. His uncanny ability to connect with his readers through wit, humor, and wisdom is a vital lifeline to today's postmodern reader. His integrity and research are an integral part of connecting today's generation with the vividly brilliant Albert Einstein."

—**Mark A. Spence, Dean of Students, School of Biblical Evangelism**

Einstein, God, and the Bible is a timely book on a subject that interests multitudes throughout the world. Ray Comfort has an exceptional gift in that he takes the most interesting subjects and creates engaging and accessible work that appeals to novice readers and scholars alike. I am sure *Einstein* will influence millions."

—**Greg Elsasser, *The Adventures of Roman and Jorge***

EINSTEIN

GOD

& THE BIBLE

EINSTEIN
GOD
& THE BIBLE

RAY
COMFORT

 WND Books

EINSTEIN, GOD, AND THE BIBLE

WND Books
Washington, D.C.

Copyright © 2014 Ray Comfort

Published by WND Books®, Washington, D.C. WND Books is a registered trademark of WorldNetDaily.com, Inc. ("WND")

Scripture quotations marked AMP are taken from the AMPLIFIED BIBLE: OLD TESTAMENT ©1962, 1964 by Zondervan (used by permission); and from THE AMPLIFIED BIBLE: NEW TESTAMENT © 1958 by the Lockman Foundation (used by permission). Scripture quotations marked ESV are from THE ENGLISH STANDARD VERSION. © 2001 by Crossway Bibles, a division of Good News Publishers. Scripture quotations marked KJV are taken from the King James Version (public domain). Scripture quotations marked KJ 2000 are taken from The King James 2000 Bible, copyright © Doctor of Theology Robert A. Couric 2000, 2003. Used by permission. All rights reserved. Scripture quotations marked NKJV are taken from the NEW KING JAMES VERSION. © 1982 by Thomas Nelson, Inc. Used by permission. All rights reserved.

Book designed by Mark Karis

WND Books are distributed to the trade by:
Midpoint Trade Books, 27 West 20th Street, Suite 1102
New York, New York 10011

WND Books are available at special discounts for bulk purchases. WND Books, Inc., also publishes books in electronic formats. For more information call (541) 474-1776 or visit www.wndbooks.com.

Hardcover ISBN: 978-1-936488-17-9
eBook ISBN: 978-1-936488-18-6

Library of Congress catalog-in-publication data available upon request.

Printed in the United States of America
14 15 16 17 18 19 XXX 9 8 7 6 5 4 3 2 1

Dedication

To Jeff and Diane Seto

"I want to know how God created this world. I am not interested in this or that phenomenon, in the spectrum of this or that element. I want to know His thoughts; the rest are details.[1]"

~ *Albert Einstein*

· Table of Contents ·

• Acknowledgments •

My sincere thanks to copy editor Renee Chavez, production coordinator Aryana Hendrawan, and the entire WND Books team, for having the vision to publish this series of books.

KEN HAM

*I*N THE PROPAGANDA WAR carried out today by the "angry atheists" (as they have been dubbed), their standard-bearer is often the late great scientist Albert Einstein. In fact, why not use him as their poster boy, the atheists would argue, if he was the smartest man in the world of the past century and also an atheist? After all, if the most brilliant man in the world was an atheist, then shouldn't all of us be smart enough to follow him and be atheists ourselves? Einstein is depicted in a well-circulated montage of photos as the most famous atheist of all. He is the logical icon for atheism—that is, if he were actually an atheist.

This fascinating new book by Ray Comfort examines that urban myth, and along the way pops other balloons in the atheists' propaganda parade.

Over the years, I have observed that an increasing number of atheist academics are no longer content with just writing books and articles in their cozy offices or speaking in the comfort of their classrooms. They have become zealots for their belief system, which is, after all, their religion. (Yes, atheism is a worldview that, along with its sister belief system, evolution, claims to explain everything around us.) Atheists are now venturing into the culture with a much greater zeal for their message, and they can put passive Christians to shame. "The new atheists," as they have been labeled, are aggressively targeting you and your children with their message. Ultimately, they want to convert you away from your faith to theirs!

Accordingly, more and more atheists are trying to persuade people of the "virtues" of atheism. One of the most outspoken of this new breed of atheists is the vehement anti-creationist Prof. Richard Dawkins, formerly of Oxford University in England. Atheists like him are not just publicity seekers who are chasing the dollar. They are very serious about their mission. It is not uncommon for Dawkins to travel to America as a crusader who preaches his atheist message in lecture halls, on TV programs, to newspaper reporters, on websites, and wherever he can.

Most Americans still believe in God, even if they

don't accept the God of the Bible or embrace the full authority of His Word. Now, if America generally believes in God, have the atheists and other secularists really had an impact on America? Well, consider the 1950s. If someone said to you back then: "The homosexual movement is on the march, and if we don't do something, 'gay' marriage will be legalized across the country," that person would have been laughed at. Almost all Americans living in the '50s believed that marriage was one man for one woman. They never would have believed that biblical marriage ever would be challenged. In the 1960s, however, atheists got prayer removed from America's government schools. In more recent decades, they have managed to get Nativity scenes taken down from public places, Ten Commandment displays removed, creation pulled out of school curricula, and so on.

Why are the atheists gaining ground? What has happened in the culture to make this possible? As the authority of God's Word and its absolutes have been undermined in America, the ideas of secular humanism and its anti-Christian messages have taken their place and have gained prominence. As I have been saying for decades, there's been a change in this culture—at a very foundational level. Generations have been indoctrinated by the secular education system and the media to build their thinking on human reason alone, not the Word of God. And at the foundation of this monumental shift has been the creation-evolution issue.

Evolutionary indoctrination has produced generations of people who now doubt God's Word beginning in Genesis, and many of these Bible-doubters are sitting in our churches. Barna Research discovered that, of teenagers today who call themselves born-again Christians, only 9 percent believe there is such a thing as absolute truth.[1] These young people are ripe for atheist evangelists like Dawkins.

Dawkins insists that Christians have no right to teach religious "nonsense" to their children. He states in his book *The God Delusion* that children who are being brought up in Christian homes are being exposed to an "infection" or a virus.[2] He has also declared that mild pedophilia is less of a kind of child abuse than telling children about the possibility of Hell![3]

One of Dawkins's "evangelistic" talks in America was actually given in a packed church, the First Parish Church in Cambridge, Massachusetts! A news report about Dawkins's message in this church stated: "At first his words are greeted with laughter, and then with resounding applause."[4] Yes, inside a church! What times we now live in!

As the authority of God's Word and its absolutes have been undermined in America, including inside the church, the ideas of secular humanism and its anti-Christian messages have gained prominence.

I praise the Lord for Christian leaders like Ray Comfort who boldly proclaim the truths of the Bible. He engages the culture and compromising churches to return to the authority of God's Word. With militant atheists increasingly on the march, Christians like Ray are needed more than ever to counter the atheist advances. We need many more churches and ministries equipping their people with resources to defend their faith and to encourage them to visit places like the Creation Museum and the future evangelistic Noah's Ark south of Cincinnati that defend the truths of God's Word.

The attacks on Christianity will probably escalate, especially since our government-run schools and secular media are promoting an anti-Christian worldview with greater fervor.

Have you ever thought: why are atheists even devoting so much time to fighting Someone they say does not exist? In their worldview, atheists must see their efforts as ultimately meaningless and a waste of their time. In fact, why do atheists like Dawkins give meaningless talks at meaningless conferences, given on a meaningless planet in a meaningless universe?

In fact, why did Dawkins help start a summer retreat in the United Kingdom for nonbelievers, ages eight to seventeen, if all is meaningless and purposeless in this world?[5]

Of course, atheists would claim they have some purpose and meaning in their actions, such as their devotion in countering what they call the myth of God's existence. But even that effort is a subjective one, and it ultimately comes from their own opinion and from no absolute authority or standard.

So why are atheists shaking their fists at God? The Scripture tells us why: they "suppress the truth in unrighteousness" (Romans 1). Basically, it comes down to the fact that they don't want to have to answer to Anyone. They want to set their own rules. Most atheists don't have a problem aborting babies or making marriage whatever they want it to be. They want to do what is "right" in their own eyes! The idea of a Creator who owns them, to whom they owe their existence, and against whom they have rebelled is anathema to them!

It baffles the mind why these atheists even bother to try to convert people to their meaningless religion. After all, what's the point? Why even go to the effort of using Einstein as their standard-bearer, even if he were an atheist?

The only explanation of why they would even bother to become evangelists for their faith is if they are engaged in a spiritual battle. Otherwise they wouldn't care. They know in their hearts there is a God, and they are deliberately suppressing that truth, as the Scripture so clearly tells us in Romans 1.

We certainly need to pray for atheists and for those people they are leading into an eternity separated from God. Indeed, God will give them what they want: separation from Him for eternity. Pray along with me and Ray that they will repent before a Holy God and receive the free gift of salvation. The Bible teaches, "If you confess with your mouth the Lord Jesus and believe in your heart that God has raised Him from the dead, you will be saved" (Romans 10:9).

After reading Ray's book, you should make it a point to share your faith with an atheist or agnostic. Did you know that the cofounder of the modern creation movement, Dr. John Whitcomb, shared the Christian faith with Einstein? Dr. Whitcomb was a student at Princeton University in the 1940s, where Einstein taught at the time. A campus ministry sponsored the showing of a film called *The God of Creation*. The elderly Einstein attended and was given a gospel tract by Dr. Whitcomb. If a young Christian like John Whitcomb could share the gospel with the smartest man on earth, what is keeping us from doing the same?

Einstein did believe in the existence of God. (Ray will prove that.) But Einstein did not, to our knowledge, ever believe in the God of the Bible. Some atheists, after reading select quotes by Einstein, attempt to argue that he was an atheist. But as Ray shows, unless Einstein repented near the end of his life, Einstein didn't believe in a *personal* God.

No, you don't have to be an Einstein to know that the evolution belief system is bankrupt scientifically. The interpretation of the evidence that atheists use in their attempt to support molecules-to-man evolution is fraught with problems. (See articles by our AiG scientists at www.AnswersInGenesis.org.)

My good friend Ray Comfort may not have an IQ as high as Einstein's, though he is sharp. (And if Ray had white hair, there might be a resemblance!) But I know that Ray would give up an IQ point for any extra dose of wisdom—wisdom that would be derived from his study and acceptance of the Word of God.

I trust you will become wiser in the things of God as you read Ray's book.

~ Ken Ham

Introduction

I N R E C E N T Y E A R S we have seen a concerted attack on the credibility of Christianity. The "new" atheists have become best-selling authors on the New York Times Best Seller list. Their open agenda is to show that Bible believers aren't intellectual, and that those who believe in creationism are nothing but simple-minded knuckle-draggers.

From the moment Albert Einstein came into a place of eminence, he became public domain. He was hounded by both theist and atheist as to his beliefs in the existence of God. Decades later he is still public domain, and he is still used as an intellectual measurement in an intense tug-of-war.

Whose side was he on? Did he believe in God or didn't he? Theists provide a mass of quotes to show that he did believe in the existence of God, but atheists are quick to retort that it wasn't the God of the Bible, inferring that he was an atheist, and they believe they have gained ground by saying so.

According to *Forbes.com*:

> In addition to name recognition and broad appeal, deceased celebrities offer the marketing community something living entertainers do not: peace of mind. "Albert Einstein isn't going to get busted for drunk driving and Steve McQueen is not going to have an affair and be in the tabloids," says David Reeder, vice president of Corbis' GreenLight, which represents Einstein, McQueen and many others. Anything that's happened is behind them, making them a safe harbor for advertisers.[1]

More than sixty years after his death, Einstein's image brings in a massive $10 million each year. Today he is more than a German-born theoretical physicist, more than just another dead celebrity or philosopher and author. He is more than the most influential and best-known scientist of all time; he is iconic.

I have a Facebook page dedicated to thousands of atheists who don't pull any punches by reminding me that I am no genius. But like a prizefighter, my bruises are a status symbol. I'm happy to report that atheist Richard Dawkins not only called me an "idiot" on CNN, but publicly called me "an ignorant fool" and a "flat-earther." But when an atheist wrote and said that I had little in common with Albert Einstein, that blow hurt, *because it's just not true.*

Einstein was Jewish; I am Jewish. He was a German Jew; my great-grandfather was a Polish Jew. We both immigrated to the United States. He believed that we were intelligently designed by God; so do I. We are both regularly misquoted by atheists. We both have moustaches (I now have a beard). We both kept our hair as age encroached, and mine has been known to look like his after a restless night's sleep.

Many times I have been told that I look like Albert Einstein. A few years ago when I was in a Phoenix airport, boarding a flight to Los Angeles, I gave one of our popular million-dollar-bill tracts to four Muslim women and a little girl who was traveling with them.[2] They were grateful and told me that I looked like Einstein.

As they passed me when boarding the plane, I heard them say, "There's Einstein." I have to say it sure made me feel good. An hour or so later, when we landed in Los Angeles, the little girl walked past my seat and said in a friendly (and loud) voice, "Good-bye, Frankenstein."

My talented son-in-law even wrote a song about

me, in which was the line "When you see a man riding a boy's bike; when you see an Einstein look-alike . . ."

There's only one thing in which I believe I trump the man, and it has nothing to do with intellect. In 1982, by the grace of God, I discovered something that is infinitely more important and has far greater repercussions than the general theory of relativity.[3] So I think I have more in common with the great genius than most.

Oh, there is one other thing that doesn't really need to be said. When it comes to brainpower, I'm not worthy to wash his socks. Actually, he didn't wear socks. But that's just one more fascinating fact about this colorful, witty, and humorous German Jew whose name is synonymous with "genius."

I hope you enjoy reading this book as much as I did writing it.

Best wishes.

~ Ray Comfort, May 2010

EINSTEIN'S HISTORY: THE EARLY YEARS

There are only two ways to live your life.
One is as though nothing is a miracle. The
other is as though everything is.[1]

—Albert Einstein

LBERT EINSTEIN was born in Germany on March 14, 1879, to Hermann and Pauline Einstein. Einstein's father was an engineer and salesman, his mother a homemaker who enjoyed playing the piano.

Even as a young child, Albert showed an amazing perception of the world around him. At the age of four, when his father showed him a pocket compass, he immediately realized there must have been something causing the needle to move.

As he grew Albert kept to himself, rarely saying a word. When he did open his mouth, he spoke slowly, often playing out entire sentences in his mind before saying them. He did this until about age nine, causing his parents to think he was mentally challenged.

One night while sitting at the dinner table, he boldly said, "The soup is too hot." His parents, pleased to hear him speak, asked why he had never said a word before. Albert replied, "Because up to now everything was in order."[2]

As a young man Albert studied in Switzerland at the Swiss Federal Polytechnic. None of his professors could have dreamed that this twenty-one-year-old would one day rise to the intellectual status he did. Though he worked hard in the lab, he hated the lectures and often missed them. His professors thought he was a loser.

During this period the handsome young Einstein often played his violin for groups of ladies at the Swiss Polytechnic. It is here that he met his future wife, Mileva Marić, also enrolled at the Polytechnic. Mileva, a mathematics and physics student, was the only woman in the academic class. Over the next few years, their friendship grew stronger and budded into a mature relationship. In a letter to her in 1900, Einstein referred to her as "a creature who is my equal and who is as strong and independent as I am."[3] She became pregnant by him the next year.

Because of his unexceptional academic record (he was notorious for skipping class), after he graduated Einstein found it extremely difficult to find employment. He became so desperate for work that he even considered leaving the world of science and becoming an insurance salesman instead. At a particularly low point in his life, he wrote in a letter to his family that perhaps it would have been better if he had never been born.

He eventually found employment as a substitute teacher and performed other temporary jobs, but his father, dissatisfied with these, stepped in and applied for academic positions on behalf of his misfit son. Sadly, in 1902 Hermann Einstein died believing that Albert was a disgrace to the family name.

Extremely depressed, Albert moved to Bern, Switzerland, and was hired as a patent clerk in the Swiss patent office. His job was to check patents and speed up the process by stripping them down to their essence, sharpening his skills as a physicist. This wasn't a demanding job, so it gave the young Einstein time to contemplate the universe—and daydream.

That same year

> Mileva gave birth to a daughter at her parents' home in Novi Sad. This was at the end of January, 1902 when Einstein was in Berne. It can be assumed from the content of the letters that birth was difficult. The girl was probably Christianized. Her official first name is unknown. In the letters received only the name "Lieserl" can be found. The further life of Lieserl is even today not totally clear. Michele Zackheim concludes in her book *Einstein's Daughter* that Lieserl was mentally challenged when she was born and lived with Mileva's family. Furthermore she is convinced that Lieserl died as a result of an infection with scarlet fever in September 1903. From the letters mentioned above it can also be assumed that Lieserl was put up for adoption after her birth. In a letter from Einstein to Mileva from September 19, 1903, Lieserl was mentioned for the last time. After that nobody knows anything about Lieserl Einstein-Maric.[4]

Einstein never saw his child.

The relationship between Albert and Mileva caused great stress to Einstein's parents, particularly his mother, and the birth of the child didn't soften the hostility. In a letter she poured out her heart to a friend: "We strongly oppose the liaison of Albert and Miss Maric . . . We don't want ever to have anything to do with her and . . . there is constant friction with Albert because of it. This Miss Maric is causing me the bitterest hours of my life. If it were in my power, I would make every possible effort to banish her from our horizon."[5]

At one point, when visiting his family's home in Milan, Albert wrote to Mileva: "Mama often cries bitterly and I am not given a single undisturbed moment here. My parents mourn for me almost as if I had died. Again and again they wail to me that I brought disaster upon myself by my engagement to you."[6]

Despite the hostility, Einstein and Mileva were married in January 1903.

***

The year 1905 has been called Einstein's "miracle year." It was then that he published four papers. The first one looked at the profound and fundamental question of the nature of life. In the second, he explored the existence of atoms—something that was virtually unknown at that time.

In the spring, Einstein was traveling by bus through Bern when he looked back at the town's clock tower. The young, aspiring physicist began to daydream about what would happen if the bus were racing through the town at the speed of light. He was astonished to realize that if he *were* traveling at the speed of light, the clock's hands would appear to be frozen in time. He later wrote that as that thought came, it was as if a storm broke loose, and thoughts began to flood his mind. This event sparked Einstein's special theory of relativity, the subject of his third paper, which maintains that space and time are very closely connected—that they are, in fact, one and the same thing: a flexible fabric called "space-time." Einstein believed he had discovered a secret of the universe.

His fourth paper that year expounded his famous $E = mc^2$—an equation that, at the simplest level, shows that energy can become matter, and matter can become energy. The tiniest speck of matter, he propounded, held a potentially massive amount of energy. To unleash it would trigger a nuclear reaction—the sort of energy we see going on in stars of the night sky. Einstein equated it to the "engine" that gives light to the stars.

When Einstein submitted the paper expounding this thought to Europe's science journals, there was little reaction because he was a mere patent clerk, and he once again became very depressed.

In time, however, his submissions fell into the

hands of one man who had the ability to fully understand them—Max Planck, the respected German physicist and editor of the most important physics journal of that time. Planck immediately recognized that this was a very important paper from the mind of a brilliant man . . . who worked at a patent office, and who still couldn't further his career as a scientist.

This same year, 1905, Albert and Mileva had a son, Hans Albert, and the family moved into a small, two-room apartment in the Swiss capital.

***

In 1907, Albert began to write a new article on his relativity theory. Over the previous couple of years, he had pondered the place of gravity in special relativity. He wanted to expand his theory of *special* relativity into a theory of *general* relativity so he would be able to explain time and gravity.

The twenty-eight-year-old patent office worker soon began to realize that what he was pondering contradicted the findings of his hero, Sir Isaac Newton. Newton was called the *founder* of modern science, and it was almost anathema to challenge him. The man whose words were the foundation of universal physics said that if an object falls, it was because there was a mysterious force drawing it to the ground.

Einstein disagreed.

One day, as he looked out the window of his patent office, he began to daydream about what would happen if a man fell off a roof. He realized that as he fell, he would be weightless. Then he imagined the man being in an elevator, and both he and the elevator falling at the same time. It would be as though gravity had been switched off. Einstein then surmised that there was no such thing as gravitational pull, but rather, the earth had curved space around us, and space was *pushing* us down. This was a completely new gravitational theory. He later recounted, "I was sitting in a chair in the patent office at Bern, when all of sudden a thought occurred to me: 'If a person falls freely he will not feel his own weight.' I was startled. This simple thought made a deep impression on me. It impelled me toward a theory of gravitation."[7]

In 1910, Albert and Mileva's second son, Eduard, was born in Zurich. Mileva had herself wanted to be a physicist, but she had failed her papers. Still, the young mother shared her husband's passions, so she assisted him and encouraged him in his own work.

In 1911, Albert Einstein was offered a position as a full-time scientist at the University of Zurich. At the age of thirty-two, he finally left the patent office and became a full-time professor. Soon he began to receive invites to attend the Solvay Conferences that brought together the greatest scientific minds in Europe. The conferences were hosted by Ernest Gaston Joseph Solvay, a well-known Belgian chemist, industrialist, and philanthropist. Einstein was the youngest professor there, and he left a great impression. He was friendly, funny, and extremely intelligent. His lectures became the talk of scientific Europe, and he was invited to speak in Berlin, Germany. Einstein hadn't visited his native country since he'd left it at age fifteen to avoid the draft. At sixteen, he had renounced his citizenship.

While Albert was in Berlin, he met a cousin he hadn't seen for years—Elsa Einstein. Elsa was completely different in character from Albert's wife, and though she wasn't interested in science, Albert liked her company. When he returned to Zurich, he continued to connect with her through letters.

Albert Einstein struggled for four years to develop his theory of general relativity. It was so complex, few people could understand it. He was aware that his theory wouldn't be accepted until he could demonstrate it. Suddenly, he had a thought. If he could shine a beam of light through an area where space is curved, then if his theory were true, the beam of light would appear to bend. He surmised that the sun had such a powerful gravitational pull that it could bend light. He believed that during a total solar eclipse, it was possible to see light bending around the sun.

Einstein turned to astrophysics for help. In 1912, he published a paper and pleaded with astronomers to observe an eclipse, but there was little reaction, and he was frustrated by the lack of response. However, one young astrophysicist, named Erwin Freundlich, was willing to work on the theory. The two met and planned to observe a total solar eclipse, which would be in Russia on August 21, 1914. Freundlich then contacted William Campbell, a pioneer of eclipse photography.[8] Campbell could see the potential of what Einstein was suggesting.

Meanwhile, Einstein's original mentor, Max Planck, was asked by the kaiser of Germany to recruit Europe's best scientists for a new institution in Berlin. Planck recommended the young Einstein.

On July 11, 1913, Planck arrived in Zurich, hoping that a personal appeal to Einstein would persuade him to return to his German homeland. He offered him a professorship in the Prussian Academy of Sciences—*the very ones who had ignored him for years were now pleading with him to take the greatest job imaginable.* At the same time his cousin wrote to him and also asked him to return to Germany.

Einstein told Planck to take a long walk, and said he would meet him at the train station. If he was carrying red roses, he told Planck, he would go to Germany. If the roses were white, he would stay in Switzerland.

He showed up at the station with red roses. Einstein had decided to follow Planck to the land of his birth.

EINSTEIN'S YEARS
OF HOPE

"Learn from yesterday, live for today, hope
for tomorrow. The important thing is to not
stop questioning."

—Albert Einstein

B Y APRIL 1914 things were looking
up for Albert Einstein. By now he was
working with elite scientists in Berlin,
and soon a solar eclipse would confirm his general
theory of relativity . . .

But his marriage was falling apart.

One eminent scientist, Fritz Haber (the institute's director), hosted Einstein's wife and two children while she looked for an apartment for the family. He noticed that the couple's relationship was disintegrating.

Einstein had, in fact, given his wife an ultimatum. In a contract headed "Conditions," he'd made the following demands:

> A. You will make sure:
>
> > 1. that my clothes and laundry are kept in good order;
> >
> > 2. that I will receive my three meals regularly *in my room*;
> >
> > 3. that my bedroom and study are kept neat, and especially that my desk is left for *my use only*.
>
> B. You will renounce all personal relations with me insofar as they are not completely necessary for social reasons.[1]

He further demanded, "You will stop talking to me if I request it."[2] Amazingly, she accepted the conditions.

Einstein later wrote to his wife again, to make sure she grasped that their relationship was going to be all business in the future, and that the "personal aspects must be reduced to a tiny remnant. In return," he vowed, "I assure you of proper comportment on my part, such as I would exercise to any woman as a stranger."[3]

It was one step further toward the downfall of the marriage. Fritz Haber tried to hold the Einsteins together, but his efforts were in vain. Tragically, in time, the couple decided to separate.

Einstein then cut another bargain with his wife. He confidently said that one day he would win a Nobel Prize, and promised her the money from it if she would give him a divorce. This would make her very wealthy, he said. Mileva agreed to the terms.

Meanwhile Erwin Freundlich and William Campbell left by train for Russia to obtain photos of the solar eclipse to attempt to prove Einstein's theory. They took four large cameras and set up in two different places so that if bad weather foiled their efforts in one location, they could still obtain photos from the other. Freundlich set up in the southeastern part of Crimea, while Campbell set his cameras in Kiev. Both parties were nervous because there were very real rumors of a coming world war.

On June 28, 1914, Archduke Franz Ferdinand of Austria was assassinated. When the German kaiser declared war on Russia, Einstein had no way to warn his colleagues of their danger. While Freundlich was setting up his cameras in the forests of Crimea, soldiers approached him and asked for his papers. When they discovered that Freundlich and his companions were Germans—with a telescope—they believed they were spies. They confiscated Freundlich's equipment and arrested him as a prisoner of war. He and his team spent months in prison.

But Campbell was an American and was considered neutral, so the Russians allowed him to keep his cameras. It made no difference: clouds obscured the eclipse, and the mission was a total failure. Campbell's remaining equipment was seized, and he returned to America a depressed and defeated man.

For Einstein, the whole adventure was an absolute disaster. He couldn't prove his most revolutionary theory of relativity.

William Campbell independently dedicated himself to Einstein's project, but because Albert was a German and they were on different sides of the war, he now looked upon Einstein as the enemy. Worse, the scientific institute in which Einstein had become involved turned its efforts toward fighting the war. He was horrified to learn that many of his old colleagues had begun to explore ways to efficiently kill people. Fritz Haber was one of the first to develop terrible weapons in the name of science. In fact, early in the war, Haber's weapon of mass destruction—a cloud of poisonous gas—was released on troops, and thousands died a horrible death in front of his eyes. Their lungs filled with liquid, and they, in essence, cruelly drowned in their own fluids. Einstein considered him to be a madman.

Deeply disgusted that scientists would use their profession to kill human beings, Albert resolved to become a pacifist. Because of his stand, he was rejected by his colleagues. At the same time, his marriage was breaking up and he was fighting a custody battle for his beloved children. To cope with the stress, he threw himself into his work.

As he looked closely at his labors, he realized that he was mistaken in his equation regarding the bending of light. He had been pushing for astrophysicists to photograph a solar eclipse, and had considered the trip to do so in Russia a complete failure. But at this revelation he had second thoughts. After recalculating his equation he became aware that, had the photography gone ahead, it might have proved him to be in error and destroyed his career.

He retreated further into his work, also spending time playing Mozart's music on his violin. This helped him concentrate on his problem. His motivation wasn't only for the progress of science—he wanted the Nobel Prize, not just for its prestige, but for the money he had promised to Mileva and his two sons.

Before the divorce was finalized the year before, his relationship with his oldest son had turned sour. Earlier in the separation, Hans Albert, affectionately nicknamed Adu, had pleaded with his father to visit him and his younger brother in Zurich for spring vacation: "Dear Papa," he wrote, "Imagine, Tete [Eduard] can already multiply and divide, and I am doing gometetry [geometry], as Tete says. Mama assigns me problems; we have a little booklet; I could do the same with you then as well. But why haven't you written us anything lately? I just think: 'At Easter you're going to be here and we'll have a Papa again.' Yours, Adu!"[4]

But the war made it virtually impossible for Einstein to visit, and though letters from Einstein to his son revealed a deep love for him, their relationship died. Albert and Mileva continued to send letters to each other, arguing about finances and vacation timing.

Then Albert received a postcard from his son, responding to his father's question about his availability for a proposed summer vacation. It coldly read:

Dear Papa,

You should contact Mama about such things, because I'm not the only one to decide here. But if you're so unfriendly to her, I don't want to go with you either. We have plans for a nice stay that I'd only give up very reluctantly. We are going at the beginning of July and are staying the whole vacation. Yours, A. Einstein.[5]

Einstein was convinced that his wife was poisoning his beloved son's attitude toward him and that Mileva was dictating the postcards. Heartbroken, he wrote to a friend:

> Just now I received the enclosed letter from my Albert, which upset me very much. After this, it's better if I don't take the long trip at all rather than experience new bitter disappointments. The boy's soul is being systematically poisoned to make sure that he doesn't trust me. Under these conditions, by attempting any approaches I harm the boy indirectly.[6]

The following Easter, Albert made it to Zurich to visit his boys. They were delighted to see him. Afterward, he wrote a note of thanks to Mileva for making things go so smoothly: "My compliments on the good condition of our boys," he said. "They are in such excellent physical and mental shape that I could not have wished for more. And I know that this is for the most part due to the proper upbringing you provide them. I am likewise thankful that you have not alienated me from the children. They came to meet me spontaneously and sweetly."[7]

Not long after, Einstein took his oldest son alone on a hike, and in a postcard to his cousin Elsa, he wrote: "My dear Elsa, Yesterday I went on a hike with the boy and am enjoying very much being with him. He is kindhearted, trusting, and surprisingly eager to learn, and intelligent. My relationship with him is becoming very warm. Kisses from your, Albert."[8]

Their "warm" relationship was short-lived.

***

In 1915, Einstein was asked to present his theory of general relativity to the most important of German scientists, at the prestigious Prussian Academy.[9] Yet, after years of work, his theory was still unproven and its mathematics appeared to be defective. He just *had* to prove the curvature of space. He canceled invitations to speak elsewhere so he could concentrate all his efforts on solving the problem.

But Einstein did accept an invitation from the University of Göttingen to use as a dress rehearsal for his presentation at the Prussian Academy. As he described his problem to a class, a mathematician named David Hilbert believed he could solve the quandary.[10] When Einstein returned to Berlin, Hilbert continued to try to solve the problem himself.

A frustrated Einstein came back to a discarded

equation that he had worked on three years earlier, and amazingly both he and David Hilbert solved the problem at the same time. Hilbert graciously gave Einstein the credit. They had found what they believed was the final equation for the general theory of relativity—just in time for Einstein's presentation at the Prussian Academy.

In 1916, he published his hypothesis. But he desperately needed photographs of a solar eclipse to prove his general theory of relativity. Unfortunately, Berlin was war-ravaged. Even the basic necessities were hard to come by, let alone the sophisticated equipment needed for photographing the sun.

Then, in the middle of a very cold winter, Albert became deathly sick. He wasn't eating, he couldn't sleep, and he soon had a complete physical and mental breakdown:

> It was an excruciating period. His marriage to Mileva Maric, an intense and brooding Serbian physicist who had helped him with the math of his 1905 paper, had just exploded. She had left him in Berlin and moved to Zurich with their sons Hans Albert, 11, and Eduard, 5. Suffering from acute stomach pains exacerbated by the food shortages of World War I, he was being nursed by a first cousin, Elsa Einstein.[11]

Albert moved into a small apartment in Berlin, where Elsa became his personal nurse. He eventually moved in with her, and she continued to care for him, eventually becoming his second wife.

Meanwhile, a brilliant astronomer at Cambridge University in England, Arthur Eddington,[12] became interested in Einstein's theory. His interest grew after he received several letters and essays on the topic from another astronomer, Willem de Sitter. Eddington had been isolated in England because he vehemently opposed the war against Germany. When he learned that Einstein also opposed the war, he saw it as an opportunity to prove that scientists across enemy lines can support each other, even in times of war. He saw Einstein's general theory as the most important scientific discovery since Newton, and wanted to show that an Englishman could stand up for a German.

The next full eclipse was to be in June of 1918, and it would be seen in the state of Washington—the home state of William Campbell. But Campbell had abandoned his cameras in Russia when the war began. Now he scrambled to find replacements, and with substandard equipment he prepared himself for the eclipse.

The night began with dense clouds, and it seemed that he was going to get a repeat of the failed Russian expedition, when suddenly, just before the eclipse, the clouds parted. Einstein's theory could be tested!

Einstein had predicted that the warped space that surrounded the sun would create the appearance that the stars around it had changed their position—they would appear to move outward. He had been extremely precise in his prediction.

But when Campbell closely examined the results of the experiment, he discovered to his disappointment that his photographic plates appeared to show that the theory of general relativity was mistaken.

Meanwhile, the war had restricted Einstein to Germany. He couldn't leave. But he did hear that Eddington was traveling to Africa to film a solar eclipse, expected on May 25, 1919. After ten weeks of traveling by ship, Eddington arrived at his destination, and he and his team spent a month building a telescope in the middle of the African jungle.

It was raining on the day of the eclipse, but amazingly, there was a gap in the clouds, and he was able to photograph the solar eclipse. Though clouds had obscured the sky in almost all of his pictures, a few plates did show the eclipse.

About this time Campbell arrived in London, carrying the results of his experiment in Washington State. He then stood before his peers at the Royal Astronomical Society and reluctantly said that Albert

Einstein was wrong.

Suddenly, the session took a spectacular turn when a cable was read from Eddington announcing *positive* results. Campbell immediately sent an urgent cable to his colleagues in the United States. It simply said, "Delay publishing Einstein results. Campbell."[13]

On November 6, 1919, Eddington arrived in London to address the Royal Astronomical Society. There was massive public interest. He revealed that his findings proved Einstein to be right! A forty-two-year-old Albert Einstein suddenly shot to an iconic status.

Still, many scientists doubted the validity of the theory of general relativity, and Einstein was exposed to increasing criticism. The test would have to be redone to verify the results.

In 1921 Einstein finally received his long-coveted Nobel Prize—but it wasn't for his still-controversial theory of relativity. It was "for his services to Theoretical Physics, and especially for his discovery of the law of the photoelectric effect."[14] Still, it was the *Nobel*, and Albert Einstein was propelled to superstardom. Instantly he was an international phenomenon. The new age of film and still-photographic carried his image worldwide and made him a household name. And now, free at last to leave Germany, he boarded a ship to the United States. The newspapers, reporting that the famous scientist was on his way to America, stirred massive public curiosity. By the time he arrived, there was so much interest in this unassuming German scientist that fifteen thousand people were waiting to meet him in Lower Manhattan.

Sadly, after winning the Nobel Prize and getting the money, Einstein broke his promise to Mileva, giving his ex-wife access only to the interest, not the principal, of the prize money. Once again, the father-son relationship with Hans Albert further soured. His elder son blamed his father entirely for leaving his mother. The feud only grew worse when his dad later objected to Hans Albert marrying the woman he loved, the opinionated Frieda Knecht:

> In fact, Einstein opposed Hans's bride in such a brutal way that it far surpassed the scene that Einstein's own mother had made about Mileva . . . Hans, at age 23, fell in love with an older and—to Einstein—unattractive woman. He damned the union, swearing that Hans's bride was a scheming woman preying on his son. When all else failed, Einstein begged Hans to not have children, as it would only make the inevitable divorce harder.[15]

Hans Albert had then immigrated to the United States, where he became a professor of hydraulic engineering at UC Berkeley, in California. Years later, even when both father and son were living in America, they remained estranged. When Einstein died in 1955, he left very little of his wealth to his son.

***

In the wake of the criticism directed at Einstein following Eddington's announcement that Einstein's theory of general relativity had been proven correct, scientists learned that there was to be another fully visible solar eclipse in Western Australia in September 1922. With Einstein's theory in mind, William Campbell redesigned his equipment and traveled to Australia. Seven other official expeditions were sent to Australia to film the eclipse, but Campbell was more experienced and better prepared than the other photographers and this time obtained many very clear photos. They confirmed, without doubt, Einstein's theory. It was a proud moment for Campbell and he immediately sent a cable to Albert Einstein.

This was also a wonderful triumph for Einstein. More than fifteen years after he first began work on his theory, he was vindicated.

He received the Copley Medal from the Royal Society in 1925. But even that was just the beginning of Einstein's superstardom.

EINSTEIN'S BELIEF
IN GOD

I cannot imagine a God who rewards and
punishes the objects of his creation and is
but a reflection of human frailty.[1]

—Albert Einstein

HROUGHOUT HIS LIFE AND CAREER,
Einstein often talked about his belief in
God's existence. This may have been
because it was a subject about which the world continually inquired. People wanted to know what the

world's most intelligent man believed about the existence of a Creator.

Although he clearly didn't believe in a *personal* God (as revealed in the Bible), Einstein wrote that he wanted to know "His" thoughts, referred to God as "He," and acknowledged that He revealed "Himself." So, it is clear *from his own writings* that he didn't believe the Creator of the universe was simply an unthinking "force." He gave God a *gender,* and he asked how God "*created* this world." In other words, it is evident that Albert Einstein wasn't a pantheist (one who thinks that God and nature are one and the same). Neither did he profess atheism, of which he is often accused by atheists. The following quotes make the point (all emphasis is added). He said:

- "I want to know how God created this world. I am not interested in this or that phenomenon, in the spectrum of this or that element. I want to know *His* thoughts; the rest are details."[2]

- "God does not care about our mathematical difficulties; *He* integrates empirically."[3]

- "My religion consists of a humble admiration of the illimitable superior Spirit who reveals *Himself* in the slight details we are able to perceive with our frail and feeble mind."[4]

- "About God, I cannot accept any concept based on the authority of the Church. As long as I can remember, I have resented mass indoctrination. I do not believe in the fear of life, in the fear of death, in blind faith. I cannot prove to you that there is no personal God, but if I were to speak of *him*, I would be a liar. I do not believe in the God of theology who rewards good and punishes evil. My God created laws that take care of that. *His* universe is not ruled by wishful thinking, but by immutable laws."[5]

- "Every one who is seriously involved in the pursuit of science becomes convinced that a spirit is manifest in the laws of the Universe—a spirit vastly superior to that of man, and one in the face of which we with our modest powers must feel humble."[6]

- "God does not play dice with the world."[7]

- "Subtle is the Lord, but malicious *He* is not."[8]

The faith of some of the more crusading fundamental atheists was no doubt bolstered by a letter Einstein wrote in which he said, "The word God is for me nothing more than the expression and product of human weaknesses, the Bible a collection of honorable, but still primitive legends. No interpretation no matter how subtle can (for me) change this."[9] It is being heralded by some as evidence for a denial of the existence of God, but the letter was consistent with the beliefs Einstein held throughout his life. He had previously stated, "I have repeatedly said that in my opinion the idea of a personal God is a childlike one."[10] The reason the name God was just a word to him was because Einstein believed He was simply unknowable. He was, in fact, angered by those who alleged that he was an atheist, saying, "In view of such harmony in the cosmos which I, with my limited human mind, am able to recognize, there are yet people who say there is no God. But what really makes me angry is that they quote me for the support of such views."[11]

In his book *The God Delusion,* atheist Richard Dawkins did precisely what angered Einstein in saying that he was an atheist.[12] When asked if he had a belief in God, Einstein replied, "I am not an atheist."[13] He even said, "The fanatical atheists . . . are like slaves who are still feeling the weight of their chains which they have thrown off after hard struggle. They are creatures who—in their grudge against traditional religion as the 'opium for the people'—cannot bear the music of the spheres."[14] Despite this, fanatical atheists still claim him as one of their own. An undeterred Richard Dawkins said, "Along with various other sources, this letter finally confirms that Einstein was, in every realistic sense of the word, an atheist."[15]

So why is there any argument as to whether or not Einstein was an atheist? It's clear he wasn't. We will look in depth at *what* he believed about God later in this book. As for why so many atheists claim him as their property, they do so because what he *did* believe is extremely meaningful. Most atheists maintain that "intelligent design" isn't intelligent, and that anyone who believes that God exists hates science.

The word *cosmos* comes from the Greek word *kósmos*, and it means "order, form, arrangement, the world or universe." Just as every arrangement of music has an arranger, this world has One who orchestrated it. That's just common sense.

Take, for instance, the dawning of an average spring day. The birds blissfully sing as the sun rises over the vast ocean's curved horizon. The air is fresh and clean. This is because without the heat of the sun, the temperature of the night air drops, then coagulates into moisture (gaining mass) and falls through the air, cleansing it of impurities—and at the same time providing moisture for the soil.

As the massive sun lifts off the ocean, it does so a moment later than it did on the previous morning, lengthening the day as summer approaches. But this isn't the only sunrise that is taking place on this day. At any moment of any day, somewhere around the earth, this same sunrise scenario is taking place. It is a perpetual occurrence. Every moment of every day, 24 hours a day, 365 days a year, the sun is rising somewhere. Yet at the same time, somewhere in the world the same sun is perpetually setting.

There is such harmony, such incredible precision in the cosmos that we can predict the exact moment of the sunrise and the sunset of any location on earth, many years into the future. For example, in Honolulu, Hawaii, on January 18, 2050, the sun will rise at 7:11 a.m. and set at 6:13 p.m. On November 6, 2063, New York City will see the sun rise at 6:32 a.m.[16] Such predictions are only possible because of the synchronization of creation. It is perfectly orchestrated.

This harmony also exists in the seasons that faithfully come around each year. At the same moment that the coolness of fall is changing the color of the leaves in the United States and ending their life, spring is causing the leaves on the trees in New Zealand to bud and break into new life. Like sunrise and sunset, fall, spring, summer, and winter are perpetually happening every moment of every day of every year on this great earth.

Harmony also exists in the clouds that form in the sky. They predictably drop their rain, then they re-form as the water of the earth evaporates and ascends into the heavens. All this happens to keep the air clean and to give the earth and its inhabitants life.

So how could any rational, thinking person believe that all this happened by chance, from nothing? Einstein believed in God as being the initial Cause, so why do we have a rise in skeptics?

An atheist who was offended by the fact that I had a picture of Einstein in the header on my blog, wrote:

> It appears dishonest in nature to do what you are doing with his photo and quotes on your blog, especially when you have been told time and again his views are not congruent with your own. How about this quote from Einstein: "It was, of course, a lie what you read about my religious convictions, a lie which is being systematically repeated. I do not believe in a personal God and I have never denied this but have expressed it clearly. If something is in me which can be called religious then it is the unbounded admiration for the structure of the world so far as our science can reveal it.

In 1945 a Navy ensign wrote to Einstein and said, "I had quite a discussion last night with a Jesuit-educated Catholic officer . . . He said that you were once an atheist. Then, said he, you talked with a Jesuit priest who gave you three syllogisms which you were unable to disprove; as a result of that you became a believer in a supreme intellect which governs the universe."[17] Einstein wrote back:

> I have never talked to a Jesuit priest in my life and I am astonished by the audacity to tell such lies about me. From the viewpoint of a Jesuit priest I am, of course, and have always been an atheist. Your counter-arguments seem to me very correct and could hardly be better formulated. It is always misleading to use anthropomorphical concepts in dealing with things outside the human sphere—childish analogies. We have to admire in humility the beautiful harmony of the structure of this world as far as we can grasp it. And that is all.[18]

The Navy ensign answered, "You say that 'From the viewpoint of a Jesuit priest I am, and have always been, an atheist.' Some people might interpret that to mean that to a Jesuit priest, anyone not a Roman Catholic is an atheist, and that you are in fact an orthodox Jew, or a Deist, or something else."[19] Einstein replied, "I have repeatedly said that in my opinion the idea of a personal God is a childlike one. You may call me an agnostic, but I do not share the crusading spirit of the professional atheist whose fervor is mostly due to a painful act of liberation from the fetters of religious indoctrination received in youth."[20]

It seems that the ensign had rightly interpreted Einstein's words that *from the view of a Jesuit priest, he was an atheist.* However, if you want to see prime examples of the quote taken out of context (quote-mining), do a search of atheist websites on the Internet. Here is the quote I have on my blog alongside the picture of a young Albert Einstein: "In view of such harmony in the cosmos which I, with my limited human mind, am able to recognize, there are yet people who say there is no God. *But what really makes me angry is that they quote me for the support of such views.* "[21]

Here again is well-known atheist professor Richard Dawkins, doing exactly what made Einstein "really angry"—portraying him as an atheist, when in truth, Einstein was no fool: "Einstein sometimes invoked the name of God (*and he is not the only atheistic scientist to do so*), inviting misunderstanding by supernaturalists eager to misunderstand and claim so illustrious a thinker as their own."[22]

In light of Einstein's "I am not an atheist,"[23] it is nothing short of deceitful to say of him, "He is not the only atheistic scientist to do so."

Einstein also battled with "fanatical atheists" in his day who were also deaf to "the music of the spheres." He said:

I was barked at by numerous dogs who are earning their food guarding ignorance and superstition for the benefit of those who profit from it. Then there are the fanatical atheists whose intolerance is of the same kind as the intolerance of the religious fanatics and comes from the same source. They are like slaves who are still feeling the weight of their chains which they have thrown off after hard struggle. They are creatures who—in their grudge against the traditional "opium for the people"—cannot bear the music of the spheres. The Wonder of nature does not become smaller because one cannot measure it by the standards of human moral and human aims.[24]

After a letter was found, apparently written by Einstein, affirming his conception of God and his belief that the Bible is a primitive legend written by human hands, atheists were a little delirious with excitement. One wrote:

Einstein was an atheist. [God's name used in blasphemy], I'm so scared this will turn out to be a forgery, but let's hope not. I mean, it makes perfect sense that Einstein would have been an atheist, but he's been held up by religious people as a "good" guy who said all the right things about how God is real and great and the universe is beyond comprehension, that part of me has bought into it. Maybe he issued pandering statements in public but felt differently in private? But what really makes this letter awesome is that he doesn't play around.

"The word God is for me nothing more than the expression and product of human weaknesses, the Bible a collection of honorable, but still primitive legends which are nevertheless pretty childish. No interpretation no matter how subtle can (for me) change this," he wrote in the letter written on January 3, 1954 to the philosopher Eric Gutkind, cited by *The Guardian* newspaper . . . "For me the Jewish religion like all others is an incarnation of the most childish superstitions," he said. "And the Jewish people to whom I gladly belong and with whose mentality I have a deep affinity have no different quality for me than all other people." Please let this be true. It's just so awesome.[25]

When I said that Einstein was no "fool," I was referring to Psalm 14:1: "The fool has said in his heart, 'There is no God.' They are corrupt, they have done abominable works, there is none who does good" (NKJV). The Amplified Bible translates the first part of this verse, "The [empty-headed] fool has said in his heart, There is no God." The Hebrew word for "fool" is לָבָנ. Its transliteration is nabal (pronounced "naw-bawl"). It means "a vile person," someone who is "foolish," "senseless," "stupid," and "wicked." The verse is referring to those who profess to be atheists—those who look at this incredible creation (all that is made) and say that they have no belief in a Maker. That is the epitome of empty-headedness, stupidity, senselessness, and in the light of the God-given conscience, wickedness.

Atheists and self-styled "freethinkers" often deceitfully use Einstein's own words to make the case that he was an atheist:

> Albert Einstein is sometimes claimed by religious theists seeking the authority of a famous scientist for their theistic views, but Einstein denied the existence of the traditional concept of a personal god. Was Albert Einstein therefore an atheist? From some perspectives his position would be seen as atheism or no different from atheism. He admitted to being a freethinker, which in a German context is much the same as atheism, but it's not clear that Einstein disbelieved in all god concepts.[26]

But the phrase "He admitted to being a freethinker" flies in the face of Einstein's own words:

> The idea of a personal God is quite alien to me and seems even naive. However, I am also not a "Freethinker" in the usual sense of the word because I find that this is in the main an attitude nourished exclusively by an opposition against naive superstition. My feeling is insofar religious as I am imbued with the consciousness of the insufficiency of the human mind to understand deeply the harmony of the Universe which we try to formulate as "laws of nature." It is this consciousness and humility I miss in the Freethinker mentality.[27]

You will find Albert Einstein listed on the website Celebrity Atheists[28] (along with several quotes on how he believed in the existence of God—that they no doubt hoped that none of their readers would notice), and in Positive Atheism's "Big List of Albert Einstein Quotations."[29] You will also find him on Atheist Empire's "Great Minds Quotes," along with his famous face to add credibility.[30] His own "I'm not an atheist," and "I want to know [God's] thoughts; the rest are details," and (in reference to being called an atheist) his statement of "But what really makes me angry is that they quote me for the support of such views" are of little consequence.

Such is the prize of Einstein.

WHY DID EINSTEIN
EMBRACE SPINOZA'S GOD?

> All religions, arts and sciences are branches
> of the same tree. All these aspirations are
> directed toward ennobling man's life, lifting
> it from the sphere of mere physical existence
> and leading the individual towards freedom.[1]
>
> —Albert Einstein

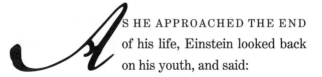

S HE APPROACHED THE END of his life, Einstein looked back on his youth, and said:

When I was a fairly precocious young man the nothingness of the hopes and strivings which chases most men restlessly through life came to my consciousness with considerable vitality. Moreover, I soon discovered the cruelty of that chase, which in those years was more carefully covered up by hypocrisy and glittering words than is the case today. By the mere existence of his stomach everyone was condemned to participate in that chase. Moreover, it was possible to satisfy the stomach by such participation, but not man in so far as he is a thinking and feeling being. As the first way out there was religion, which is implanted into every child by way of the traditional education-machine. Thus I came—despite the fact that I was the son of entirely irreligious (Jewish) parents—to a deep religiosity.[2]

However, this "deep religiosity" was qualified. He said, "I believe in Spinoza's God, who reveals Himself in the lawful harmony of the world, not in a God Who concerns Himself with the fate and the doings of mankind."[3] He added, "I am fascinated by Spinoza's pantheism, but I admire even more his contribution to modern thought because he is the first philosopher to deal with the soul and body as one, and not two separate things."[4] He even wrote a poem about him:

How much do I love that noble man

More than I could tell with words

I fear though he'll remain alone

With a holy halo of his own.[5]

In a letter written to Murray W. Gross, dated April 26, 1947, he said:

> It seems to me that the idea of a personal God is an anthropomorphic concept which I cannot take seriously. I feel also not able to imagine some will or goal outside the human sphere. My views are near to those of Spinoza: admiration for the beauty of and belief in the logical simplicity of the order and harmony which we can grasp humbly and only imperfectly. I believe that we have to content ourselves with our imperfect knowledge and understanding and treat values and moral obligations as a purely human problem—the most important of all human problems.[6]

Spinoza[7] believed that God exists only philosophically and that He is abstract and impersonal. Einstein's belief in the god of Spinoza seems to have been sparked back in 1921:

> While the argument over his birthday present had been going on, the theory of relativity had been used to pull him into a religious controversy from which there emerged one of his much-quoted statements of faith. It began when Cardinal O'Connell of Boston, who had attacked Einstein's General Theory on previous occasions,

told a group of Catholics that it "cloaked the ghastly apparition of atheism" and "befogged speculation, producing universal doubt about God and His Creation." Einstein, who had often reiterated his remark of 1921 to Archbishop Davidson—"It makes no difference. It is purely abstract science"—was at first uninterested. Then, on April 24, Rabbi Herbert Goldstein of the Institutional Synagogue, New York, faced Einstein with the simple five-word cablegram: "Do you believe in God?"

"I believe in Spinoza's God who reveals himself in the orderly harmony of what exists," he replied, "not in a God who concerns himself with fates and actions of human beings."

Years later he expanded this in a letter . . . "I can understand your aversion to the use of the term 'religion' to describe an emotional and psychological attitude which shows itself most clearly in Spinoza," he wrote. "[But] I have not found a better expression than 'religious' for the trust in the rational nature of reality that is, at least to a certain extent, accessible to human reason."[8]

When author Edward Busching sent Einstein a copy of his book *Es Gibt Keinen Gott* [*There Is No God*], in a letter dated October 25, 1929, he responded that the book only dealt with the concept of a personal God, and said:

We followers of Spinoza see our God in the wonderful order and lawfulness of all that exists and in its soul ("Beseeltheit") as it reveals itself in man and animal. It is a different question whether belief in a personal God should be contested. Freud endorsed this view in his latest publication. I myself would never engage in such a task. For such a belief seems to me preferable to the lack of any transcendental outlook of life, and I wonder whether one can ever successfully render to the majority of mankind a more sublime means in order to satisfy its metaphysical needs.[9]

In an essay called "The World as I See it," Einstein wrote:

Everything that the human race has done and thought is concerned with the satisfaction of felt needs and the assuagement of pain. One has to keep this constantly in mind if one wishes to understand spiritual movements and their development. Feeling and desire are the motive forces behind all human endeavor and human creation, in however exalted a guise the latter may present itself to us. Now what are the feelings and needs that have led men to religious thought and belief in the widest sense of the words? A little consideration will suffice to show us that the most varying emotions preside over the birth of religious thought and experience. With primitive man it is above all fear that evokes religious notions—fear of hunger, wild beasts, sickness, death. Since at this stage of existence understanding of causal connexions is usually poorly developed, the human mind creates for itself more or less analogous beings on whose wills and actions these fearful happenings depend. One's object now is to secure the favour of these beings by carrying out actions and offering sacrifices which, according to the tradition handed down from generation to generation, propitiate them or make them well disposed towards a mortal.[10]

Einstein is of course correct when he says that no sane person seeks unhappiness and desires pain. Most religions believe in human guilt, and that in turn leads to a fear of some sort of punishment. Fear does evoke "religious notions." Man creates religions to deal with his guilt because he fears some sort of divine retribution. He also has fears of hunger, sickness, and death, which further steer him toward the divine to seek peace through good works or some sort of religious sacrifice. The professor continues:

I am speaking now of the religion of fear. This, though not created, is in an important degree stabilized by the formation of a special priestly caste which sets up as a mediator between the people and the beings they fear, and erects a hegemony on this basis. In many cases the leader or ruler whose position depends on other factors, or a privileged class, combines priestly functions with its secular authority in order to make the latter more secure; or the political rulers and the priestly caste make common cause in their own interests.[11]

It would seem that Einstein is addressing the priestly hierarchy of established religion, who teach that you and I cannot approach God without their mediation. It is not clear whether he is referring to a particular church, but it is known that he received his elementary education at a Roman Catholic school:

> When Albert turned 6 and had to go to school, his parents did not care that there was no Jewish one near their home. Instead he went to the large Catholic school in their neighborhood, the Petersschule. As the only Jew among the seventy students in his class, Einstein took the standard course in Catholic religion and ended up enjoying it immensely. Indeed, he did so well in his Catholic studies that he helped his classmates with theirs ... Einstein avoided religious rituals for the rest of his life ... He did, however, retain from his childhood religious phase a profound reverence for the harmony and beauty of what he called the mind of God as it was expressed in the creation of the universe and its laws.[12]

When asked by an atheist if he were, in fact, deeply religious, Einstein replied, "Yes, you can call it that. Try and penetrate with our limited means the secrets of nature and you will find that, behind all the discernible concatenations, there remains something subtle, intangible and inexplicable. Veneration for this force beyond anything that we can comprehend is my religion. To that extent I am, in point of fact, religious."[13]

Even though the Catholicism gave him an appreciation of God's creation, this didn't stop him from speaking out about their policies. He wrote, "I am convinced that some political and social activities and practices of the Catholic organizations are detrimental and even dangerous for the community as a whole, here and everywhere. I mention here only the fight against birth control at a time when overpopulation in various countries has become a serious threat to the health of people and a grave obstacle to any attempt to organize peace on this planet."[14] He also said, "The minority, the ruling class at present, has the schools and press, usually the Church as well, under its thumb. This enables it to organize and sway the emotions of the masses, and make its tool of them."[15]

Einstein maintained that it is through this "need" for their mediation that they maintain control of their millions. Why does it work so well? He tells us why:

> The social feelings are another source of the crystallization of religion. Fathers and mothers and the leaders of larger human communities are mortal and fallible. The desire for guidance, love, and support prompts men to form the social

or moral conception of God. This is the God of Providence who protects, disposes, rewards, and punishes, the God who, according to the width of the believer's outlook, loves and cherishes the life of the tribe or of the human race, or even life as such, the comforter in sorrow and unsatisfied longing, who preserves the souls of the dead. This is the social or moral conception of God.[16]

True, human beings are dying, and we are prone to error. We are lost and we need love and guidance. It is therefore comforting to have a God who provides an answer to death and who "protects, rewards, and punishes." It is comforting to believe that we are loved and have a purpose in existence. This isn't just a concept of God most human beings have and need, but it is the concept of God revealed in the Bible. Watch now what Einstein does:

The Jewish scriptures admirably illustrate the development from the religion of fear to moral religion, which is continued in the New Testament. The religions of all civilized peoples, especially the peoples of the Orient, are primarily moral religions. The development from a religion of fear to moral religion is a great step in a nation's life. That primitive religions are based entirely on fear and the religions of civilized peoples purely on morality is a prejudice against which we must be on our guard. The truth is that they are all intermediate types, with this reservation, that on the higher levels of social life the religion of morality predominates.[17]

While Einstein was Jewish by birth, he didn't embrace Judaism. He said, "I am a determinist. I do not believe in free will. Jews believe in free will. They believe that man shapes his own life. I reject that doctrine. In that respect I am not a Jew."[18] He, for some reason, believed that the Jewish Scriptures (the Old Testament) move from a religion of fear (by which he was offended), to a "moral religion," which he said continues in the New Testament.

As much as I admire and respect the man, Einstein was in error. His summation of "The development from a religion of fear to moral religion is a great step in a nation's life"[19] may be the way nations often take, but the Bible has never moved away from teaching that God is to be feared. This is true both in the Old and in the New Testaments. When God gave the Ten Commandments, the Israelites were so fearful they thought they would die, and they pleaded with Moses to have God not speak to them directly:

> And all the people saw the thunderings, and the lightnings, and the noise of the trumpet, and the mountain smoking: and when the people saw it, they removed, and stood afar off. And they said to Moses, You speak with us, and we will hear:

> but let not God speak with us, lest we die. And
> Moses said unto the people, Fear not: for God
> is come to prove you, and that his fear may be
> before your faces, that you sin not. (Exodus
> 20:18–20 KJV)

That was in the Old Testament, when He came in peace to give His Law. When He comes in wrath to judge those who have transgressed His Law, the Bible warns in the *New* Testament, they will drink the wine of His wrath: "And to you who are troubled rest with us, when the Lord Jesus shall be revealed from heaven with his mighty angels: In flaming fire taking vengeance on them that know not God, and that obey not the gospel of our Lord Jesus Christ: Who shall be punished with everlasting destruction from the presence of the Lord, and from the glory of his power . . ." (2 Thessalonians 1:7–9 KJV).

So it is with this erroneous presupposition that Einstein said, "I cannot conceive of a God who rewards and punishes his creatures, or has a will of the kind that we experience in ourselves. Neither can I nor would I want to conceive of an individual that survives his physical death; let feeble souls, from fear or absurd egoism, cherish such thoughts."[20]

Einstein could not conceive of a God who rewards and punishes humanity. He rejected the notion that

we are created in His image, with a moral choice—
a free will. Then he said something that flies in the face
of common sense. He said he didn't want to conceive
anyone living forever, and called those who have a will
to live "feeble souls." Then I gladly align myself with
feeble souls. I want to live forever, and deeply cherish
the thought that I have everlasting life in Christ.

It seems that Einstein believed we should surrender to the power of death. The Bible, on the other
hand, teaches that death is an enemy: "For [Christ]
must reign, till he has put all enemies under his feet.
The last enemy that shall be destroyed is death" (1
Corinthians 15:25–26 KJV). Einstein considered those
who fight death to be weak, and those who surrender
to the enemy to be strong. Yet the fear of death is not
a bad thing. Fear stops us from getting too close to a
cliff's edge. Fear also makes me put on a parachute
before a jump. Certain fears are not to be feared;
they are to be embraced. Those who fear death seek
life. Those who don't yield to its power. Who then are
the feeble folk?

Einstein also considered those who seek immortality to be motivated by "absurd egoism." I wonder
if he forgot his previous admonition: "The important
thing is not to stop questioning. Curiosity has its
own reason for existing. One cannot help but be in

awe when he contemplates the mysteries of eternity, of life, of the marvelous structure of reality. It is enough if one tries merely to comprehend a little of this mystery every day. Never lose a holy curiosity."[21] Didn't he exercise holy curiosity as to why a man dies, and the possibility of his immortality? Or did his exploration stop at the pages of Holy Scripture? Where was his curiosity when it came to the most important of life's issues? Did the professor not care for himself? Did he have no sense of self-worth or of self-preservation? To want to live forever is an intuitive instinct given to us by God.

Einstein said that he was "satisfied with the *mystery* of the eternity of life."[22] There is no "mystery" at all for those who obey the gospel. They know the truth and the truth makes them free.

He also maintained that he was happy to have a "glimpse of the marvelous structure of the existing world, together with the devoted striving to comprehend a portion, be it ever so tiny, of the Reason that manifests itself in nature."[23] How tragic. Seeing God's creation should have steered him to the Creator. Instead he saw nature as an end to itself. With that thought in mind, look at how Holy Scripture shows the progression of those who give themselves to the lusts of their hearts, and how they give homage to nature (the creature) rather than to God: "God also gave them up to uncleanness through the lusts of their own hearts, to dishonour their own bodies between themselves: who changed the truth of God into a lie, and worshipped and served the creature more than the Creator, who is blessed for ever. Amen" (Romans 1:24–25 KJV).

We often overlook the power of belief. But what we believe does matter. If I arrived home one night believing that a man with a gun had broken into my home, that belief would govern my actions. I would immediately call the police. If I didn't believe there was a dangerous and armed man in my house, I would enter it without fear. Belief would direct my steps. Einstein didn't "believe in immortality of the individual [soul], and," said he, "I consider ethics to be an exclusively human concern with no superhuman authority behind it."[24]

Why would any individual seek immortality if he was convinced there was no such thing? It makes sense to close the mind if one is convinced otherwise. Again, this flies in the face of Einstein's want to learn—his holy curiosity.

Why would Einstein abandon the God of his fathers? Why would he, in the light of the horrific holocaust endured by his own people, not want to embrace the God who wrote in stone, "Thou shalt not kill"? Surely a Jew would take great consolation in a God who will see to it that a mass murderer such as Adolf Hitler will be given ultimate and divine justice. His words make no sense. The equation is wrong. He reasoned:

Nobody, certainly, will deny that the idea of the existence of an omnipotent, just, and omnibeneficent personal God is able to accord man solace, help, and guidance; also, by virtue of its simplicity it is accessible to the most undeveloped mind. But, on the other hand, there are decisive weaknesses attached to this idea in itself, which have been painfully felt since the beginning of history. That is, if this being is omnipotent, then every occurrence, including every human action, every human thought, and every human feeling and aspiration is also His work; how is it possible to think of holding men responsible for their deeds and thoughts before such an almighty Being? In giving out punishment and rewards He would to a certain extent be passing judgment on Himself. How can this be combined with the goodness and righteousness ascribed to Him?

The main source of the present-day conflicts between the spheres of religion and of science lies in this concept of a personal God.[25]

If a judge passes sentence on a heinous criminal, he's not passing judgment on himself. His judgment reveals that the judge is good, and that he upholds the principle of civil law. God does not impugn Himself by upholding righteousness. He reveals Himself as just and good.

Einstein once said, "The highest principles for our aspirations and judgments are given to us in the Jewish-Christian religious tradition. It is a very high goal which, with our weak powers, we can reach only very inadequately, but which gives a sure foundation to our aspirations and valuations."[26] Yet, the Law of God is the very core of the Jewish tradition. The Ten Commandments are the backbone for their aspirations and judgments. They tell us right from wrong, the likes and dislikes of the One who created us.

The real problem for Einstein was that there was more than one commandment. The God who immutably said, "Thou shalt not kill," also said, "Thou shalt not commit adultery." So why would a Jew refuse to believe in a God who rewards and punishes His creatures? Perhaps the following quotes reveal why:

> When Albert admitted adultery and divorced Mileva in 1919, he promised that in the event he should win the Nobel Prize all the money—not part of the money but all the money—would go to Mileva.[27]

Einstein's marriage to Marić ended in acrimony. He began treating Marić, for whom he had originally professed such great love, cruelly toward the end of the marriage, even calling her "uncommonly ugly" (see *Collected Papers*). He admitted in a deposition during divorce proceedings (28 December 1918) that he had carried on an adulterous relationship with one of his cousins, whom he later married. During this second marriage, Einstein had numerous affairs, even including—apparently—an affair with a Russian spy! And again, Einstein never breathed a word about having fathered a daughter with Marić.[28]

Documents show the twentieth-century giant was generous, affectionate, and adulterous . . . Previously released letters suggested that his first marriage was miserable, and that he cheated on Elsa with his secretary, Betty Neumann . . . Einstein was surprisingly candid to Elsa about his extramarital affairs. Between the mid-1920s and his emigration to the US in 1933, there were several women in his life: a Margarete, an Estella, two women called Toni and an Ethel . . . Einstein wrote to the son of a friend who had died: "What I admire in your father is that, for his whole life, he stayed with only one woman. This is a project in which I grossly failed, twice."[29]

A reviewer of the book *Einstein's Mistakes: The Human Failings of Genius*[30] said:

> The book also explores Einstein's intimate relationships—his adulteries, divorce, and relationship with his children. We learn that his greatest motive for leaving Zurich in 1914 to teach at the Prussian Academy of Sciences in Berlin was the possibility of an adulterous liaison with Elsa, his double cousin (a cousin both on his mother's and father's side), whom he eventually married (but not before he made a pass at her 20-year-old daughter, Ilse). In discussing these relationships, Ohanian reveals Einstein's unattractive and at times cruel side. Einstein's memo to his first wife Mileva ". . . reads like a set of orders issued by a Prussian officer to his batman," he writes. "What makes this memo even uglier is the undercurrent of hypocrisy that runs through it. Einstein acts as though *he* were the offended party, and that Mileva was guilty of adultery or some worse offense." Some of Einstein's letters to Mileva are included, as are his letters to Elsa.[31]

How true it is that men love darkness rather than light: "For everyone practicing evil hates the light and does not come to the light, lest his deeds should be exposed" (John 3:20). Any god will do, as long as it's not the God who said, "You shall not commit adultery."

EINSTEIN'S "FAITH IN GOD IS CHILDLIKE"

It is easier to denature plutonium than to denature the evil spirit of man.

—Albert Einstein

*A*N ATHEIST ONCE WROTE to me and asked, "Do you agree with Einstein that your faith in God is a childlike one?" This question is more than likely a reference to Einstein's "The word god is for me nothing more than the expression and product of human weaknesses, the Bible a collection of honourable, but still primitive legends which are nevertheless pretty childish. No interpretation no matter how subtle can (for me) change this."[1]

I agree partly with Einstein's view of the Bible. It does seem to be filled with stories that are pretty childish. However, there's good reason for that.

For a number of years I ran Bible clubs for kids. Hundreds would gather after school to listen to me tell them Bible stories. My granddad gave me a ventriloquist's dummy, so I used it to teach the kids. I called him "Charlie," and now and then I would tell stories and speak to the kids through him. I was the world's worst ventriloquist, but the kids didn't care.

At the end of the year, I would have a local bakery bake "the world's biggest chocolate cake" and have it carried into the club with great fanfare. Then I would let each of the kids have a huge slice. I also approached local businesses, told them what I was doing, and asked them to donate candy for the kids. After each club I would have the kids line up for a free mouthful, so not only did they learn about God and hear the gospel, but had a great time while doing it. So did I.

On one of these occasions, when about a hundred kids were lined up for candy, I noticed some of them pushing and shoving at the front of the line. I glanced to the other end and saw that those children were lining up peacefully. As I watched, I realized that I was looking at a line of greed. The greedy brats were at the front, and the quiet, sickly, humble kids were at the back.

So I did something that gave me great delight. I said, "Stay where you are. If anyone moves out of line, they won't get any candy. Now turn—about-face." All the kids obeyed, and the line turned around 180 degrees. Then I took great joy in going to the back of the line first and giving the quiet, sickly kids their candy, much to the annoyance of the brats, who were now at the back.

Have you ever noticed that in this world the proud, the confident, the good-looking, and the rich have great advantage? And the poor, the sickly, the homely, and the humble are the ones who often get trodden on? They never seem to be able to get on their feet. Meanwhile, the rich get richer by treading on the poor. If there were a line of success in this life, the rich would be at the front and the poor would be at the back. Life seems unfair.

Here now is something that gives me great delight. God, in His great wisdom, has turned the line completely around, and He did it in a way that is amazing.

Let me tell you about a soldier who had a terrible skin disease. He tried every modern remedy he could find. Nothing helped.

One day, someone spoke of a person who had a remedy in another country. The soldier traveled to this country to get an appointment, located the man's residence, and spoke to one of his assistants. He said who he was, how far he had traveled, and what he was seeking from the man.

After some time, the assistant returned and told the soldier that he should go and bathe in the local river. Then he said something that greatly annoyed the soldier. He told him that to be cured from the ailment, he had to bob up and down in the river seven times. The proud soldier was understandably angered by such stupid talk, and immediately left to go back to his home country.

This paraphrased story is from the Bible. Naaman was a captain of the Syrian Guard. He was no doubt proud and successful. But he had leprosy. When he found out that Elisha the prophet could heal the disease, he set out to visit him.

Elisha didn't even come to the door. He had his assistant tell Naaman that to be cured he had to bathe in the river Jordan seven times. Naaman was angered. He assumed that the prophet would wave his hand over him and he would be cured. Instead he was told to do this crazy thing. He was about to leave the country when someone reminded him that he had nothing to lose by obeying the prophet. He could either rot and die with incurable leprosy, or he could do what he was told.

He decided to do what Elisha said. Visualize now the scene. Naaman is a proud captain. He is with his soldiers. They watch him wade out into the Jordan River; then down he lowers himself, into the water. Once. Then twice. Three times. What he is doing is extremely humbling. Four times. He was probably thinking, *This is crazy!* Five. Six. Nothing has happened. He is still a leper. Down he goes for the last time, and up he comes out of the water, with his skin like that of a babe!

What Naaman did was childish. It was foolish. It was an insult to his intellectual dignity. But it cured his leprosy. He was cured because of his faith, his humility, and his obedience. God was the one who healed him, but the way to his healing came through the very low door of humility.

Here now is how God went to the other end of the line. He stayed with the Naaman pattern by taking the humble and weak things of this world and using them to turn the tables on the proud. He chose a seemingly foolish message as the means of giving eternal life to dying humanity. He stayed with the pattern when He chose the indignity of being born in a cow's feeding trough, riding into Jerusalem on the back of a donkey, and dying a criminal's death on a Roman cross. In reference to the birth of Christ, we are told, "He has shown strength and made might with His arm; He has scattered the proud and haughty in and by the imagination and purpose and designs of their hearts. He has put down the mighty from their thrones and exalted those of low degree" (Luke 1:51–52 AMP).

Listen to Jesus address this subject: "I thank You, Father, Lord of heaven and earth, that You have concealed these things [relating to salvation] from the wise and understanding and learned, and revealed them to babes (the childish, unskilled, and untaught). Yes, Father, for such was Your gracious will and choice and good pleasure" (Luke 10:21 AMP).

Look at the apostle Paul also speak of how God turned the line around and sent the proud and arrogant world to the back of the line:

> We preach Christ (the Messiah) crucified, [preaching which] to the Jews is a scandal and an offensive stumbling block [that springs a snare or trap], and to the Gentiles it is absurd and utterly

unphilosophical nonsense. But to those who are called, whether Jew or Greek (Gentile), Christ [is] the Power of God and the Wisdom of God. [This is] because the foolish thing [that has its source in] God is wiser than men, and the weak thing [that springs] from God is stronger than men. For [simply] consider your own call, brethren; not many [of you were considered to be] wise according to human estimates and standards, not many influential and powerful, not many of high and noble birth. [No] for God selected (deliberately chose) what in the world is foolish to put the wise to shame, and what the world calls weak to put the strong to shame. And God also selected (deliberately chose) what in the world is lowborn and insignificant and branded and treated with contempt, even the things that are nothing, that He might depose and bring to nothing the things that are, so that no mortal man should [have pretense for glorying and] boast in the presence of God. (1 Corinthians 1:23–29 AMP)

More than a thousand years before Christ, the Bible tells us that God "takes the wise in their own craftiness" (Job 5:13 KJ 2000). Paul quotes this verse when he says, "Let no man deceive himself. If any man among you seems to be wise in this world, let him become a fool, that he may be wise. For the wisdom of this world is foolishness with God. For it is written, He takes the wise in their own craftiness. And again, The Lord knows the thoughts of the wise, that they are vain" (1 Corinthians 3:18–20 KJV).

Again, I do agree in one sense with Einstein. I think that the whole Bible—from start to finish, is childish, especially the Bible stories. Think of it. If you become a believer, you will be forced to say, "I believe in Adam and Eve, Noah and the Ark, Jonah and the whale, Samson and Delilah, David and Goliath, and all the other stories related in the Scriptures."

Christianity is also childlike: "Then Jesus called a little child to Him, set him in the midst of them, and said, 'Assuredly, I say to you, unless you are converted and become as little children, you will by no means enter the kingdom of heaven'" (Matthew 18:22 NKJV). But God was simply using the Naaman pattern, and He used it from the beginning of Genesis to the end of Revelation.

If you are proud, if you have any intellectual dignity, you will never stoop (you will never lower yourself) to come to Christ. What would your friends think? How humbling it would be for you to say that you believe the Bible . . . and there is the wonderful wisdom of God. You are snared by your own sinful pride. Without childlike faith, without humility of the heart, without lowering your proud self, you will find that you will be thrust out of the very gates of heaven, and thus find yourself in hell:

Let no person deceive himself. If anyone among you supposes that he is wise in this age, let him become a fool [let him discard his worldly discernment and recognize himself as dull, stupid, and foolish, without true learning and scholarship], that he may become [really] wise. For this world's wisdom is foolishness (absurdity and stupidity) with God, for it is written, He lays hold of the wise in their [own] craftiness; and again, The Lord knows the thoughts and reasonings of the [humanly] wise and recognizes how futile they are. (1 Corinthians 2:18–20 AMP)

THE BOLD ASSERTION

My religion consists of a humble admiration
of the illimitable superior spirit who reveals
himself in the slight details we are able to
perceive with our frail and feeble mind.[1]

—Albert Einstein

HEN EINSTEIN was just
thirty-four, he boldly said,
"I have firmly resolved to bite
the dust, when my time comes, with the minimum
of medical assistance, and up to then I will sin to my

wicked heart's content."[2] Similarly, I had a friend who as a young man said that he would kill himself when he reached the age of fifty. He then threw himself into sin without restraint, and indeed, killed himself at age fifty.

Albert Einstein wasn't quite as foolhardy as my friend. He was a thinker. Time tends to make most (who think deeply about life's issues) somewhat philosophical. Just two months before his death in 1955, he contemplated: "To one bent on age, death will come as a release. I feel this quite strongly now that I have grown old myself and have come to regard death like an old debt, at long last to be discharged. Still, instinctively one does everything possible to postpone the final settlement. Such is the game that nature plays with us."[3]

The Bible says that every sane person is tormented by the fear of death. Francis Bacon said, "Men fear death as children fear to go into the dark; and as that natural fear in children is increased with tales, so is the other."[4]

How true are the words of another genius. Leonardo da Vinci said, "While I thought that I was learning how to live, I have been learning how to die." Einstein seemed to yield to death, but unwillingly. At the same time he unwittingly spoke biblical truth. It's not *nature* that seeks a "final settlement"; it is the Law of a holy God. Albert Einstein may have kept his word and sinned to his "wicked heart's content." Little did he know that God also kept His word and stored up His wrath with every sin he committed. Look at the warning of Scripture:

> But in accordance with your hardness and your impenitent heart you are treasuring up for yourself wrath in the day of wrath and revelation of the righteous judgment of God, who *"will render to each one according to his deeds"*: eternal life to those who by patient continuance in doing good seek for glory, honor, and immortality; but to those who are self-seeking and do not obey the truth, but obey unrighteousness—indignation and wrath, tribulation and anguish, on every soul of man who does evil, of the Jew first and also of the Greek; but glory, honor, and peace to everyone who works what is good, to the Jew first and also to the Greek. For there is no partiality with God. (Romans 2:2–11 NKJV; emphasis added)

Like a guilty criminal who has transgressed civil law, Albert (like the rest of sinful humanity) was deep in debt to eternal justice because he had transgressed God's Law. This great debt, of which he spoke, could not be satisfied with mere silver and gold. It was a debt that demanded capital punishment. It called for the death penalty for guilty transgressors . . . and eternal damnation in hell. Its terrible decree demands that "the soul who sins shall die" (Ezekiel 18:20 NKJV), but it is a demand that was fully satisfied by the One who cried from Calvary's cross, "It is finished!" (John 19:30 NKJV). It was paid in full by the precious blood of Jesus.

In the meantime, if Einstein wasn't an atheist, or a pantheist, and if he didn't believe in a personal God, or the God of the Jews, in what sort of deity did he believe? He continually reiterated his belief with words such as "It was, of course, a lie what you read about my religious convictions, a lie which is being systematically repeated. I do not believe in a personal God and I have never denied this but have expressed it clearly. If something is in me which can be called religious then it is the unbounded admiration for the structure of the world so far as our science can reveal it."[5]

In 1930, he stated:

> It seems to me that the idea of a personal God is an anthropological concept which I cannot take seriously. I also cannot imagine some will or goal outside the human sphere . . . Science has been charged with undermining morality, but the charge is unjust. A man's ethical behavior should be based effectually on sympathy, education, and social ties and needs; no religious basis is necessary. Man would indeed be in a poor way if he had to be restrained by fear of punishment and hope of reward after death.[6]

He also said:

The desire for guidance, love, and support prompts men to form the social or moral conception of God. This is the God of Providence, who protects, disposes, rewards, and punishes; the God who, according to the limits of the believer's outlook, loves and cherishes the life of the tribe or of the human race, or even of life itself; the comforter in sorrow and unsatisfied longing; he who preserves the souls of the dead. This is the social or moral conception of God.[7]

Then, in 1949, he repeated his beliefs that God was unknowable and again separated himself from atheism. He said:

I have repeatedly said that in my opinion the idea of a personal God is a childlike one. You may call me an agnostic, but I do not share the crusading spirit of the professional atheist whose fervor is mostly due to a painful act of liberation from the fetters of religious indoctrination received in youth. I prefer an attitude of humility corresponding to the weakness of our intellectual understanding of nature and of our own being.[8]

Einstein made a god in his own image and was in transgression of the first and the second of the Ten Commandments. "You shall have no other gods before Me," and "You shall not make unto yourself any graven image," not confined to physically shaping a stone or wooden god (Exodus 20:3 NKJV; 20:4 KJ2000). The Commandments include a god shaped in the mind. When an idolater speaks of God, he usually uses the words "my God" to describe the god that he conceived. Einstein was consistent with this expression. He said, "I do not believe in the God of theology who rewards good and punishes evil. My God created laws that take care of that. His universe is not ruled by wishful thinking, but by immutable laws."[9]

It's ironic that Einstein once said, "During the youthful period of mankind's spiritual evolution, human fantasy created gods in man's own image who, by the operations of their will were supposed to determine, or at any rate influence, the phenomenal world."

He did the very same thing![10]

There is a serious problem, though, for the idolater. By their very nature idolaters reject the God of the Bible, as the two aren't compatible. The God revealed in Scripture forbids the giving of homage to the nonexistent, and in turn, the idolater refuses to give homage to the God of Scripture.

Here's how it works. The average idol-maker is offended by the thought that God would be vindictive. He is affronted by any thought of the existence of hell. He therefore creates a god that is nonvindictive. His god is rather an impersonal but benevolent force. He has no sense of right or wrong, justice or truth. But there's the problem. This "benevolent" deity stands by and cruelly lets children starve to death—forty thousand every twenty-four hours. He lets people die in agony of cancerous diseases. Millions of them. He coldly watches as hundreds of thousands are crushed in earthquakes, drowned in floods, struck by lightning, and ravaged by tornadoes and hurricanes.

Then, as time passes, as the pains of daily life come to the individual idolater, he cannot reconcile what his benevolent god allows to come his way. So he either becomes embittered or disillusioned at the thought of God existing. He then loses faith, because his god let him down.

As we have seen earlier, just before his death Einstein said, "The word god is for me nothing more than the expression and product of human weaknesses, the Bible a collection of honourable, but still primitive legends which are nevertheless pretty childish. No interpretation no matter how subtle can (for me) change this."[11] At that point in his life, Albert Einstein rejected the God who revealed Himself in Holy Scripture, shaped an idol for himself, and then discarded it when the pains of old age took their predictable hold and pulled him closer and closer to death.

Yet, he held the answer to this dilemma in his own hands. Look at what he said about the nature of God: "I see a clock, but I cannot envision the clockmaker. The human mind is unable to conceive of the four dimensions, so how can it conceive of a God, before whom a thousand years and a thousand dimensions are as one?"[12]

So if the incredible mind of Albert Einstein couldn't begin to understand the Creator, why then did he go to the trouble of conceiving his own image of God? If the clock is complex, then the clockmaker is exponentially more complex, and if the maker is beyond comprehension, that's where trust must come in. None of us can begin to understand the Creator, so in the light of the incomprehensible complexities of creation, we should simply exercise faith and believe what the Scriptures say about Him.

Albert Einstein didn't do that. He couldn't understand how God could be a God of justice, so he created a god that was in line with his understanding, and in time it was only right that he should toss the idol. His god could do nothing for him. It was impotent . . . nothing more than an imaginary friend.

But he still wasn't an atheist.

WHY EINSTEIN WAS
NOT AN ATHEIST

I have found no better expression than
"religious" for confidence in the rational
nature of reality, insofar as it is accessible
to human reason. Whenever this feeling is
absent, science degenerates into uninspired
empiricism.[1]

—Albert Einstein

*A*S MENTIONED EARLIER, if
you search atheist websites, you
will find that many claim Ein-
stein as one of their own. This is often done by having
masses of quotes from him, giving the impression that

he and the atheists were on the same team. They were not. As we have seen, Einstein didn't believe in the God of the Bible, but he was no atheist. He made that clear. He couldn't have made it more clear than with his "I'm not an atheist." Here are his words in context when asked, "Do you believe in God?":

> I'm not an atheist. I don't think I can call myself a pantheist. The problem involved is too vast for our limited minds. We are in the position of a little child entering a huge library filled with books in many languages. The child knows someone must have written those books. It does not know how. It does not understand the languages in which they are written. The child dimly suspects a mysterious order in the arrangement of the books but doesn't know what it is. That, it seems to me, is the attitude of even the most intelligent human being toward God. We see the universe marvelously arranged and obeying certain laws but only dimly understand these laws.[2]

Einstein said:

> Speaking of the spirit that informs modern scientific investigations, I am of the opinion that all the finer speculations in the realm of science spring from a deep religious feeling, and that without such a feeling they would not be fruitful. I also believe that, this kind of religiousness, which makes itself felt today in scientific investigations, is the only creative religious activity of our time.

The art of today can hardly be looked upon at all
as expressive of our religious instincts.[3]

He also said, as you'll recall from an earlier
chapter:

I have repeatedly said that in my opinion the idea
of a personal God is a childlike one. You may call
me an agnostic, but I do not share the crusading
spirit of the professional atheist whose fervor
is mostly due to a painful act of liberation from
the fetters of religious indoctrination received
in youth. I prefer an attitude of humility corresponding to the weakness of our intellectual
understanding of nature and of our own being.[4]

The reason he refused to embrace atheism was
the fact that he saw the genius of God's creative hand
in creation: "In view of such harmony in the cosmos
which I, with my limited human mind, am able to
recognize, there are yet people who say there is no
God. But what really makes me angry is that they
quote me for the support of such views."[5]

However, a true atheist is someone who believes
that nothing created everything. Most will deny that
they believe that because it shows that atheism is not
only foolish, but unscientific. Nothing cannot create
anything. It is scientifically impossible.

Even though such a belief is ridiculous, it is held

by arguably the world's most outspoken atheist. Professor Richard Dawkins believes that nothing created everything. Here are his own words:

> If, as returning host, I reflect on this whole pilgrimage, my overwhelming reaction is one of amazement. Amazement at the extravaganza of detail that we have seen; amazement, too, at the very fact that there are any such details to be had at all, on any planet. The universe could so easily have remained lifeless and simple—just physics and chemistry, just the scattered dust of the cosmic explosion that gave birth to time and space. The fact that it did not—the fact that life evolved out of nearly nothing, some 10 billion years *after the universe evolved out of literally nothing*—is a fact so staggering that I would be mad to attempt words to do it justice. And even that is not the end of the matter. Not only did evolution happen: it eventually led to beings capable of comprehending the process, and even of comprehending the process by which they comprehend it.[6]

There are a few things that the professor and I agree on. One is that we both despise the horrible hypocrisy within organized religion and blame it for mass atrocities down through the ages, as well as rampant pedophilia among its priests. And we both can only think of two alternatives to creation. Either something created everything, or nothing is responsible.

Dawkins isn't the only one who believes that it was nothing that was responsible for creating everything:

"It is now becoming clear that everything can—and probably did—come from nothing."[7]

—Robert A. J. Matthews, physicist, Ashton University, England

"Space and time both started at the Big Bang and therefore there was nothing before it."[8]

—Cornell University, "Ask an Astronomer"

"Some physicists believe our universe was created by colliding with another, but Kaku [a theoretical physicist at City University of New York] says it also may have sprung from nothing."[9]

—Scienceline.org

"Even if we don't have a precise idea of exactly what took place at the beginning, we can at least see that the origin of the universe from nothing need not be unlawful or unnatural or unscientific."[10]

—Paul Davies, physicist, Arizona State University

"Assuming the universe came from nothing, it is empty to begin with . . . Only by the constant action of an agent outside the universe, such as God, could a state of nothingness be maintained. The fact that we have something is just what we would expect if there is no God."[11]

—Victor J. Stenger, atheist, author of *God: The Failed Hypothesis. How Science Shows That God Does Not Exist*

"Few people are aware of the fact that many modern physicists claim that things—perhaps even the entire universe—can indeed arise from nothing via natural processes."[12]

—Atheist Mark I. Vuletic

"To understand these facts we have to turn to science. Where did they all come from, and how did they get so darned outrageous? Well, it all started with nothing."

—"Fifty Outrageous Animal Facts," Animal Planet

"To the average person it might seem obvious that nothing can happen in nothing.

But to a quantum physicist, nothing is, in fact, something."

—*Discover* magazine, April 1, 2002, "Guth's Grand Guess"

"It is rather fantastic to realize that the laws of physics can describe how everything was created in a random quantum fluctuation out of nothing, and how over the course of 15 billion years, matter could organize in such complex ways that we have human beings sitting here, talking, doing things intentionally."[13]

—Alan Harvey Guth, theoretical physicist and cosmologist

The modern atheist who knows that it's unscientific foolishness to believe that nothing created anything, let alone everything, will often fall back to a couple of alternative beliefs. He will say that he believes that the universe is eternal, and that it therefore doesn't need a Maker. But he has a big problem with that belief because it's unscientific. The universe cannot be eternal. This is because of entropy (or the second law of thermodynamics). Everything is running down. It is degenerating—from the sun, to rocks, to fruit, and even your own body. If you leave an apple on your table for a month, it won't get better. It will get worse—it will rot. Everything material does. That's common knowledge and a scientific fact.

If the earth were eternal (as atheists apparently believe)—that it is multiple quattuordecillion years (plus) old, then it would have crumbled to dust trillions of years ago.

God is a Spirit (He is not material) and He is eternal—without beginning and without end, and He is the Creator of all things. He is nothing like what we conceive Him to be. He is not bound by time or space, is utterly perfect—something preachers often call "perfect holiness" (probably based on Matthew 5:48). When God spoke to Israel, they thought they were going to die, because the experience was so fearful. So we must dash any image we have of an old man in the sky, reaching out to a naked Adam. That's idolatry.

The second "alternative" for the modern atheist is to redefine words. As one atheist wrote to me:

ATHEISTS DON'T BELIEVE IN A "CRE-ATION." There is no creation! The universe wasn't created, it isn't a creation, it's just a thing. An event happened and then the universe was there, or the universe was always there, or something else, which doesn't matter. The point is, the universe wasn't created, it arose, evolved, came about by random vacuum fluctuations, what have you.

This is the sadly pathetic and unthinking nature of modern atheism. It's what it comes down to—"There's no creation." Such a philosophy is nothing but an intellectual embarrassment. This is why the title of my book *You Can Lead an Atheist to Evidence but You Can't Make Him Think* isn't just a witty book title; it's the truth. All the evidence in the world is staring at the atheist, and he gets rid of it (in his mind) by calling it "a thing." But that doesn't get rid of the Creator. He created every "thing" we can see, and everything we can't see.

There is a game that modern atheists play. It's a word game. They say, "I can't prove that Santa doesn't exist, but I have no belief that he does." Then they apply that principle to God. They don't say that He doesn't exist. They just have no belief that He does. In so doing, they cleverly outwit those who are trying to instruct them about their eternal salvation. Many Christians have no comeback with the clever atheist word game. The clever atheist is like a man who plays a game with his parachute instructor. When the instructor is looking the other way, he cuts holes in his own parachute—but he does it so that it can't be detected by his instructor.

Such can be very frustrating for those of us who want to reason with the "new" atheist. If he is asked to provide an explanation as to why he believes the unscientific thought that nonlife produced life, the modern atheist has the ultimate cop-out cut-and-paste answer. It is that he doesn't know how life came out of nonlife, and he doesn't have to know because "the beginning" doesn't concern him. It just happened, and one day science will have the answer. In the meantime, he places himself in the lofty position of not having to justify his lack of intellectual stance because he's not the one making a claim. You are. You say that God exists, so he believes that you are the one who has to provide evidential proof. And he says that he sees no evidence that God exists. That's the new and convenient definition of an atheist—someone who sees no belief that a god exists.

Then, like a dim-witted, blind, and deaf judge, he dismisses evidence put before him (such as that which has been made being axiomatic evidence for a Maker) as being laughingly inadmissible. Case dismissed. Then he, in a bizarre self-conceit, proclaims himself wise.

Such is the intellectual embarrassment of the "new" atheism. However, their brainless position isn't new at all. The Scriptures had them pegged two thousand years ago:

> For since the creation of the world His invisible
> attributes are clearly seen, being understood
> by the things that are made, even His eternal
> power and Godhead, so that they are without
> excuse, because, although they knew God, they
> did not glorify Him as God, nor were thankful,
> but became futile in their thoughts, and their
> foolish hearts were darkened. Professing to be
> wise, they became fools. (Romans 1:20–22 NKJV)

The Bible also speaks of "unreasonable" men (see 2 Thessalonians 3:20). Such can't be reasoned with, even with such simple common sense. What's more, in a further effort to fortify themselves against the truth, they twist the Scripture to mean things it doesn't say, and the tragedy is, what they do will result in their own terrible and eternal downfall: "There are some things in those [epistles of Paul] that are difficult to understand, which the ignorant and unstable twist and misconstrue to their own utter destruction, just as [they distort and misinterpret] the rest of the Scriptures" (2 Peter 3:16 AMP).

Einstein often referred to "religious instincts" that each of us has. We know intuitively that there is a Creator and that He requires moral accountability. Unreasonable men ignore and even deny this God-given inner light. In the Sermon on the Mount, Jesus addressed the inner light and warned of the consequences of ignoring it. He said, "The lamp of the body is the eye. If therefore your eye is good, your whole body will be full of light. But if your eye is bad, your whole body will be full of darkness. If therefore the light that is in you is darkness, how great is that darkness!" (Matthew 6:22–23 NKJV).

EINSTEIN'S "RELIGION"

He . . . who can no longer pause to wonder
and stand rapt in awe, is as good as dead;
his eyes are closed.[1]

—Albert Einstein

*T*HERE'S NO SUCH THING as a genuine atheist. God has given "light" to
every thinking man and woman. We are
aware of His invisible attributes—they are "clearly
seen" by the things that are made (Romans 1:20

NKJV). Nothing that has been made was "made" without a Maker. God is the Creator of all life—animate and inanimate. Nothing came into being of its own accord. Nonlife cannot give birth to life. That is a scientific impossibility.

Einstein, speaking of his "religious" convictions, said, "Try and penetrate with our limited means the secrets of nature and you will find that, behind all the discernible concatenations, there remains something subtle, intangible and inexplicable. Veneration for this force beyond anything that we can comprehend is my religion. To that extent I am, in point of fact, religious."[2] When Einstein spoke of this "subtle, intangible and inexplicable" something, he wasn't speaking from the insight of a genius. It doesn't take a rocket scientist to know that whoever or whatever made all this was incredible beyond words. Albert was simply revealing the inner light that God has given to every man.

Here's proof that he was right: When the apostle Paul arrived in Athens, his heart was stirred because the whole city was given to idolatry. They had multiple gods:

> Now while Paul waited for them at Athens, his
> spirit was stirred in him, when he saw the city

wholly given to idolatry. Therefore disputed he in the synagogue with the Jews, and with the devout persons, and in the market daily with them that met with him. Then certain philosophers of the Epicureans, and of the Stoicks, encountered him. And some said, What will this babbler say? other some, He seemeth to be a setter forth of strange gods: because he preached unto them Jesus, and the resurrection. And they took him, and brought him unto Areopagus, saying, May we know what this new doctrine, whereof thou speakest, is? For thou bringest certain strange things to our ears: we would know therefore what these things mean. (For all the Athenians and strangers which were there spent their time in nothing else, but either to tell, or to hear some new thing.) (Acts 17:16–21 KJV)

These men may seem to be rather strange. They spent all their time, like a group of nattering ladies in a knitting circle, talking about "new" things. Yet they were no different from contemporary America. We spend almost all of our time also talking about new things. We have papers that tell us the news. We have radio news reports, news flashes, nightly TV news, and new news from Hollywood. If it's new, it's news. We are probably worse than the nattering Athenians. So how did Paul address his hearers?

Then Paul stood in the midst of Mars' hill, and said, Ye men of Athens, I perceive that in all

> things ye are too superstitious. For as I passed
> by, and beheld your devotions, I found an altar
> with this inscription, To The Unknown God.
> Whom therefore ye ignorantly worship, him
> declare I unto you. (Acts 17:22–23 kjv)

Notice that Paul didn't speak of their ignorance
of the existence of God, but of their ignorance as to
His identity. Their altar was dedicated to a God they
didn't know. This is the true state of all of godless
humanity. They know He exists through creation,
but they don't know Him personally. Paul then told
the Athenians that the God of whom he was about to
speak is the Creator of all things. He made the world
and everything that dwells in it. It didn't happen by
chance. It didn't evolve over billions of years. God
created it, He is "Lord" of heaven and earth, and we
are subject to His lordship.

The apostle said:

> God that made the world and all things therein,
> seeing that he is Lord of heaven and earth,
> dwelleth not in temples made with hands; nei-
> ther is worshipped with men's hands, as though
> he needed any thing, seeing he giveth to all life,
> and breath, and all things; and hath made of
> one blood all nations of men for to dwell on all
> the face of the earth, and hath determined the
> times before appointed, and the bounds of their
> habitation; that they should seek the Lord, if

haply they might feel after him, and find him, though he be not far from every one of us: For in him we live, and move, and have our being; as certain also of your own poets have said, for we are also his offspring. Forasmuch then as we are the offspring of God, we ought not to think that the Godhead is like unto gold, or silver, or stone, graven by art and man's device. And the times of this ignorance God winked at; but now commandeth all men every where to repent: Because he hath appointed a day, in the which he will judge the world in righteousness by that man whom he hath ordained; whereof he hath given assurance unto all men, in that he hath raised him from the dead.

And when they heard of the resurrection of the dead, some mocked: and others said, We will hear thee again of this matter. (Acts 17:24–32 KJV)

There is an "ignorance" that God kindly overlooks. It is the ignorance of misguided devotion. It is not of His existence, because that "ignorance" is a willing ignorance. It is an "ignore-ance" of something that is clearly evident through the existence of creation. Einstein wasn't so foolish. He listened to his intuitive knowledge and acknowledged his Creator.

He didn't, however, acknowledge the God of whom Paul spoke. Paul preached the God of the Jews—the One who spoke creation into existence as accounted so clearly in the Jewish Scriptures. This is what Einstein said of his Jewish heritage:

> For me the Jewish religion like all others is an incarnation of the most childish' superstitions. And the Jewish people to whom I gladly belong and with whose mentality I have a deep affinity have no different quality for me than all other people. As far as my experience goes, they are no better than other human groups, although they are protected from the worst cancers by a lack of power. Otherwise I cannot see anything "chosen" about them.[3]

While Einstein may have been a genius when it came to physics, he flunked in history. If you want to know if the Jews are a chosen people, study their history. Anyone with half a mind can see that there is something very special about the Jews. They were scattered throughout the world, and yet they were able to retain their identity. Then after two thousand years of not having their own country, they gathered as one nation. America has Italians, French, Russian, and Chinese people living within it. But Italy, France, Russia and China still exist. The Jews had no home, yet there are Jews in every country in which they gathered. God preserved them and drew them back to their homeland.

They were not only preserved as a nation, but they were chosen to bring the gospel to the world. The Jews were chosen by God to bring the Messiah into the world. Of course, that's not a big deal to those who have no understanding.

If a child were to find the diary of Leonardo da Vinci, he may use it as a coloring book. He would give no value to it because he lacks understanding as to its worth. On the other hand, one of da Vinci's notebooks, the Codex Leicester, was purchased by Bill Gates for $30.8 million back in 1994. He explained why he valued the book:

> I feel very lucky that I own a notebook. In fact, I remember going home one night and telling my wife Melinda that I was going to buy a notebook; she didn't think that was a very big deal. I said, no, this is a pretty special notebook, this is the Codex Leicester, one of the Notebooks of Leonardo da Vinci. And I personally have always been amazed by him because he personally worked out science on his own, and he understood things that no other scientist of that time did.

Yet people thought Gates had lost his mind. And so it is with those who give no value to the Messiah's birth. They even mock that which is precious. However, those who understand who this was, give this event unspeakable value. This babe born in Bethlehem was God in human form—God manifest in the flesh—for the express purpose of suffering for the sins of the world, so that the door of death could be closed for humanity and the door of immortality swung open wide. Think of it—if this was the promised Messiah, if Jesus of Nazareth was God in human form, if He did take our punishment, if He can give everlasting life to all who repent and trust in Him—what better news could you hope to ever hear? And the Jews were chosen to usher in that news.

Again, in the light of Nazi Germany, Einstein made statements that make little sense. Let's revisit a quote we examined earlier:

> It seems to me that the idea of a personal God is an anthropological concept which I cannot take seriously. I also cannot imagine some will or goal outside the human sphere . . . Science has been charged with undermining morality, but the charge is unjust. A man's ethical behavior should be based effectually on sympathy, education, and social ties and needs; no religious basis is necessary. Man would indeed be in a poor way if he had to be restrained by fear of punishment and hope of reward after death.[5]

If God (or a "religious basis") is removed from the equation, society has no basis at all upon which to build an absolute morality. If we removed God's "Thou shalt not kill," who then has the authority to forbid murder? What happens if a society like Hitler's Germany legalized the liquidation of an entire race of people? Nazi Germany's "sympathy" was with the Aryan race. They educated their youth to hate Jews, and "social ties and needs" were confined to the German people. That was the law of the state. If there is no God and no moral absolutes, they did nothing wrong when they exterminated six millions Jews. It was all legal and no one has any right to protest in the slightest.

You and I know better.

ANSWERING
EINSTEIN'S
DIFFICULTIES

How strange is the lot of us mortals! Each of
us is here for a brief sojourn; for what purpose he knows not, though he senses it. But
without deeper reflection one knows from
daily life that one exists for other people.[1]

—Albert Einstein

ET'S BEGIN THIS CHAPTER by
looking again at Einstein's quote about
God's vindictive nature:

I cannot conceive of a God who rewards and punishes his creatures, or has a will of the kind that we experience in ourselves. Neither can I nor would I want to conceive of an individual that survives his physical death; let feeble souls, from fear or absurd egoism, cherish such thoughts. I am satisfied with the mystery of the eternity of life and with the awareness and a glimpse of the marvelous structure of the existing world, together with the devoted striving to comprehend a portion, be it ever so tiny, of the Reason that manifests itself in nature.[2]

In a previous chapter, we looked at Albert Einstein's unwillingness to believe in a God who holds His creation to a moral accountability. But think again of the character of such a being. Would we consider such a deity to be good or evil? What would we think of the character of any civil judge who allows heinous criminals to go free? Such a "judge" would be evil and should be brought to justice himself. If he is of good character, he must do all he can to see that justice is done. The key to understanding this is in the word *heinous*. It is understandable if a judge lets petty crimes go unpunished, but if he allowed a multi-murderous pedophile to escape justice, then the judge is no judge at all. He is evil by nature and should be removed from the bench and prosecuted himself.

So if the god that Einstein believes in refuses to punish *evident* evil and make sure that perfect justice is done, he is evil by nature. Our problem is that we don't see things such as lying, theft, lust, and greed, as heinous. God does.

Einstein also said:

> Through the reading of popular scientific books I soon reached the conviction that much in the stories of the Bible could not be true. The consequence was a positively fanatic orgy of freethinking coupled with the impression that youth is intentionally being deceived by the state through lies; it was a crushing impression. Mistrust of every kind of authority grew out of this experience, a skeptical attitude toward the convictions that were alive in any specific social environment—an attitude that has never again left me, even though, later on, it has been tempered by a better insight into the causal connections.[3]

When we deny the supernatural nature of God, the evident consequence will be that the Bible will be seen as a book of untrue stories. It's a supernatural book from beginning to end. The words "In the beginning God created the heavens and the earth" (Genesis 1:1 KJV) will be meaningless if in our minds we strip God of the supernatural. If we conceive of an impotent god who did nothing in the beginning and does nothing today, accounts of the miraculous—such as closing the mouths of His creatures, as recounted in the book of Daniel; parting seas He created; and walking on water He made—will be nothing but silly "stories."

On the other hand, if we begin with the premise that God created all things and that He can do all things, everything becomes possible. "Stories" are effortlessly believable.

> If this being is omnipotent, then every occurrence, including every human action, every human thought, and every human feeling and aspiration is also His work; how is it possible to think of holding men responsible for their deeds and thoughts before such an almighty Being? In giving out punishment and rewards He would to a certain extent be passing judgment on Himself. How can this be combined with the goodness and righteousness ascribed to Him? The main source of the present-day conflicts between the spheres of religion and of science lies in this concept of a personal God.[4]

There is a conflict with the concept of a "personal" God Himself, but it isn't a conflict with science. It is rather specifically a conflict between the Law of God and godless men who happen to be scientists. There is also a conflict between the Law of God and sinful men who are mechanics, plumbers, doctors, lawyers, and politicians. By "personal" Einstein is referring to a God who holds each of us personally accountable to His Law. That means adulterers will be held accountable. That means that murders, rapists, thieves, and liars will be held accountable, and to conceive of a god who doesn't hold men accountable is to run against our natural intuition. If God is good, He must, by His very nature, hold a wicked world accountable for wicked deeds. Look at how Romans 8:7 pinpoints the problem: "[That is] because the mind of the flesh [with its carnal thoughts and purposes] is hostile to God, for it does not submit itself to God's Law; indeed it cannot" (AMP).

The "mind of the flesh" is the biblical way of referring to the godless mind of humanity. It is a mind that is consumed with godless thoughts. Its carnal thoughts are listed in Galatians 5:18–21: "But if ye be led of the Spirit, ye are not under the law. Now the works of the flesh are manifest, which are these; adultery, fornication, uncleanness, lasciviousness, idolatry, witchcraft, hatred, variance, emulations, wrath, strife, seditions, heresies, envyings, murders, drunkenness, revellings, and such like: of the which I tell you before, as I have also told you in time past, that they which do such things shall not inherit the kingdom of God" (KJV).

Notice that those who have been regenerated by the Holy Spirit (born again—see John 3), that is, "led of the Spirit," are not under the Law of God. In other words, those who trust in the Savior are sheltered from the wrath of the just and holy Law. Those who are still in their sins are under its terrible wrath (see John 3:36).

Perhaps the most famous of Bible verses is John 3:16: "For God so loved the world, that he gave his only begotten Son, that whosoever believeth in him should not perish, but have everlasting life" (KJV). But rarely do we see the context of this verse:

> For God sent not his Son into the world to condemn the world; but that the world through him might be saved. He that believeth on him is not condemned: but he that believeth not is condemned already, because he hath not believed in the name of the only begotten Son of God. And this is the condemnation, that light is come into the world, and men loved darkness rather than light, because their deeds were evil. (vv. 17–19 KJV)

Those who fail to trust in Christ are already condemned. The Law of God proclaims them guilty of transgressing its precepts. So again, when Einstein says, "The main source of the present-day conflicts between the spheres of religion and of science lies in this concept of a personal God,"[5] the conflict is with God's Law:

To be sure, the doctrine of a personal God interfering with the natural events could never be *refuted*, in the real sense, by science, for this doctrine can always take refuge in those domains in which scientific knowledge has not yet been able to set foot.

But I am persuaded that such behavior on the part of the representatives of religion would not only be unworthy but also fatal. For a doctrine which is able to maintain itself not in clear light but only in the dark, will of necessity lose its effect on mankind, with incalculable harm to human progress.[6]

Einstein often spoke of his objection to God being personal, interfering, and judging, and his thoughts weren't at all passive. He called such interference "fatal," said it was "in the dark," and believed it would do "incalculable harm to human progress." It is clear that he is deeply offended by the thought that God would hold humanity personally responsible. But, again, he isn't alone in this feeling of offense. Look at what Jesus said about the subject: "The world cannot hate you, but it hates Me because I testify of it that its works are evil" (John 7:7 NKJV). The world hates Jesus Christ because He testifies that their works are evil. That's why His name is used as a cuss word (how much do you have to despise someone to do that?). In a sense the same thing happens between the police and the criminal. The criminal hates the officer of the law because he "testifies" that the criminal's works are evil. Many police officers have died at the hands of criminals, not because of who they are, but because of that for which they stand. They uphold the law, and that's an offense to lawbreakers.

Let's look at some more of Einstein's logic: "A conflict arises when a religious community insists on the absolute truthfulness of all statements recorded in the Bible," he said. "This means an intervention on the part of religion into the sphere of science; this is where the struggle of the Church against the doctrines of Galileo and Darwin belongs."[7]

Einstein is clearly confused as to the biblical meaning of the words "the Church." According to the Bible it's universally those who love God, irrespective of their denomination. The Church is called a number of things in Scripture—"the body of Christ," "believers," "saints," and Christians." Neither is any religious Protestant organization the "body of Christ."

It was, rather, the *Roman Catholic* Church that held back science, imprisoned Galileo, was responsible for the Inquisition (the torture of Christians), the bloody Crusades, and more. The Catholic Church is a religious organization and is not "the body of

Christ." However, those Catholics or Protestants who have repented and put their trust entirely in Jesus Christ alone for their eternal salvation are part of the body of Christ. It is an understanding of what entails the true Church that keeps the Christian from being disheartened by rampant hypocrisy. He knows that God will sort the false from the true on Judgment Day.

So Einstein's conflict (as is the conflict of many today) was more than likely with the Roman Catholic Church, with its dogmas and traditions that conflicted with the progress of science. This is what he said in that respect:

> It is this mythical, or rather this symbolic, content of the religious traditions which is likely to come into conflict with science. This occurs whenever this religious stock of ideas contains dogmatically fixed statements on subjects which belong in the domain of science. Thus, it is of vital importance for the preservation of true religion that such conflicts be avoided when they arise from subjects which, in fact, are not really essential for the pursuance of the religious aims.[8]

In April 2010, the *Sunday Times* headlined: "Richard Dawkins calls for arrest of Pope Benedict XVI. Richard Dawkins, the atheist campaigner, is planning a legal ambush to have the Pope arrested during his state visit to Britain 'for crimes against humanity.'"[9]

Dawkins sure had the big talk. In March of the same year, he asked the question, "Should the pope resign?" and answered:

> No. As the College of Cardinals must have recognized when they elected him, he is perfectly—ideally—qualified to lead the Roman Catholic Church. A leering old villain in a frock, who spent decades conspiring behind closed doors for the position he now holds; a man who believes he is infallible and acts the part; a man whose preaching of scientific falsehood is responsible for the deaths of countless AIDS victims in Africa; a man whose first instinct when his priests are caught with their pants down is to cover up the scandal and damn the young victims to silence: in short, exactly the right man for the job. He should not resign, moreover, because he is perfectly positioned to accelerate the downfall of the evil, corrupt organization whose character he fits like a glove, and of which he is the absolute and historically appropriate monarch. No, Pope Ratzinger should not resign. He should remain in charge of the whole rotten edifice—the whole profiteering, woman-fearing, guilt-gorging, truth-hating, child-raping institution—while it tumbles, amid a stench of incense and a rain of tourist-kitsch sacred hearts and preposterously crowned virgins, about his ears.[10]

The *Sunday Times* was referring to this when Dawkins apparently had linked with fellow atheist

Christopher Hitchens on a social agenda to make sure that justice was done.

The thought should make us smile because no one takes on the pope. He's too big, too powerful, too lofty, and too loved by too many for two atheists to hold him accountable for anything. It's a matter of survival of the fittest. The two outspoken atheists would be fortunate to get a balcony wave in their general direction, let alone their day in court with the pope.

Of course, it wasn't true. The good professor was all talk. He said that any talk of an arrest was an exaggeration. A misunderstanding. Media spin. Like when the missing link was found in 2009. Hype, that's all. Like when the professor said that he believed we were the products of aliens.[11] Afterwards, he said that he didn't mean that. And he didn't mean this. David didn't have a tiny stone to sling.

Richard Dawkins isn't the only evolutionary believer who also believes in the possibility of aliens. According to the *Times* online:

> The aliens are out there and Earth had better watch out, at least according to Stephen Hawking. He has suggested that extraterrestrials are almost certain to exist—but that instead of seeking them out, humanity should be doing all it . . . can to avoid any contact.

The suggestions come in a new documentary series in which Hawking, one of the world's leading scientists, will set out his latest thinking on some of the universe's greatest mysteries.

Alien life, he will suggest, is almost certain to exist in many other parts of the universe: not just in planets, but perhaps in the centre of stars or even floating in interplanetary space.[12]

So although modern evolutionary believers can see into space and believe in aliens, they can't seem to see the difference between the visible church and *the* Church, which is the body of true believers in Jesus Christ. It is this "Church"—made up of those who truly love God and obey His Word—to which Scripture refers when it says:

Husbands, love your wives, even as Christ also loved the church, and gave himself for it; that he might sanctify and cleanse it with the washing of water by the word, that he might present it to himself a glorious church, not having spot, or wrinkle, or any such thing; but that it should be holy and without blemish. (Ephesians 5:25–27)

ALBERT EINSTEIN AND THE ATOMIC BOMB

We scientists, whose tragic destination has been to help in making the methods of annihilation more gruesome and more effective, must consider it our solemn and transcendent duty to do all in our power in preventing these weapons from being used for the brutal purpose for which they were invented. What task could possibly be more important to us? What social aim could be closer to our hearts? Human beings, vegetables, or cosmic dust; we all dance to a mysterious tune, intoned in the distance by an invisible piper.[1]

—Albert Einstein

ALBERT EINSTEIN was a pacifist. It seems he didn't think too much of human nature. He said that it was easier to defuse plutonium than it was to defuse human nature. It's a time bomb waiting to go off.

While there is good in every one of us (some of the Mafia bosses are kind to their dogs), you don't have to look too far to see the evil, even from man's perspective. Families fight; neighbors fight; politicians, gangs, kids, and nations fight. If Stephen Hawking is right and there are aliens out there, if we discover them, we aren't the ones who should be concerned. The odds are that we will start a war and kill them.

In the last century there have been more than a hundred major wars, resulting in the deaths of millions of human beings.[2] The 1917–21 Soviet revolution took 5 million lives; in 1931, in the Japanese Manchurian War, 1.1 million people lost their lives; in the conflict between the Soviet Union and the Ukraine in 1932–33, there were 10 million casualties; in 1936–37, 13 million were killed in Stalin's purges; from 1939 to 1945, during the World War II era, 55 million died, including those killed in the Holocaust and in a Chinese revolution. And the list goes on.

These are just statistics, and they tend to be cold and impersonal. But think of the absolute tragedy of war—young men and women in the prime of life were killed . . . for what? Usually for dirt. Wars are fought over land. One country invades another. So people give their lives; then the blood-soaked land they fought over is returned twenty years later after peace negotiations . . . until the next war. The applicable acronym for WAR is "We Are Right."

Einstein saw through the repetitive cycle. He valued human life, and it led to his pacifism . . . until Hitler rose to power. A pacifist is someone who is strongly and actively opposed to conflict, and especially war. Almost everyone is opposed to war. We don't want our young men and women to be killed. We don't want to have to shoot or blow up another human being, but so often peace-loving people and nations are pulled into a war they didn't instigate. If a killer threatens your family, do you resist him? Do you call gun-toting police? If you had a gun, would you shoot a killer who was about to stab your child? Is your family worth protecting? How about your neighborhood or your country? These are issues that no doubt confronted an unwilling Einstein when Hitler rose to power.

Way back in 1905, as Einstein worked on the special theory of relativity, he maintained that a massive amount of energy could be released from a tiny amount of matter. This is what the equation $E=mc^2$ (energy = mass times the speed of light squared) expresses. In years to come, this principle would evidently be seen in the atomic bomb.

However, the atomic bomb wasn't what a peace-loving Albert Einstein had in his brilliant mind when he initially published $E = mc^2$. Had he known the future and how he would embrace pacifism, he probably would have abandoned this area of his work.

Later on, even as a young man, he showed his disdain for war by leaving his homeland to avoid the draft. In 1929, true to the convictions of his youth, he openly made it known that if war ever broke out, he would "unconditionally refuse to do war service, direct or indirect . . . regardless of how the cause of the war should be judged."[3]

His pacifist position changed in 1933, as he watched a madman rise to power in the form of Adolf Hitler.

Hitler's rise to political supremacy was gradual. The Great Depression of the early 1930s had brought with it Germany's economic and political collapse. Hitler took advantage of this by developing the Nazi Party, which propelled him to power.

The Nazis were able to devise an electoral strategy that won over Germany's northern farmers and white-collar workers in small towns. Hitler had made sweeping political promises, and that produced a huge victory in 1930. The Nazis then joined forces with Communists in sweeping violence across Germany from 1931 to 1933.

During that period Hitler ran for the German

presidency and was able to win 30 percent of the vote, and that had forced the eventual victor, Paul von Hindenburg, into a special runoff election. Hitler then entered a coalition government as chancellor in 1933. Then, in August of the following year, he succeeded Hindenburg after he died. Once Hitler was in a place of power, he began to crush any opponents and establish his dictatorship. As Einstein watched Hitler ascend to a place of political control and threaten European stability, he could no longer call himself an "absolute pacifist."

In 1938, Hitler seized Austria and the Sudetenland. His army then invaded Poland in 1939, causing a declaration of war on Germany by France and England. As German tanks and infantry began to sweep through the rest of Western Europe, nation after nation fell to the German war machine.

It was in 1939 that the famous "Einstein–Szilárd letter" was sent to President Franklin D. Roosevelt. It was signed by Einstein but it was mostly authored by Leó Szilárd along with fellow Hungarian physicists Edward Teller and Eugene Wigner. The letter warned the president that Nazi Germany might be researching the use of nuclear fission to create atomic bombs. The letter suggested that the United States begin its own research on the bomb. It warned:

In the course of the last four months it has been made probable—through the work of Joliot in France as well as Fermi and Szilard in America—that it may become possible to set up a nuclear chain reaction in a large mass of uranium, by which vast amounts of power and large quantities of new radium-like elements would be generated. Now it appears almost certain that this could be achieved in the immediate future.

This new phenomenon would also lead to the construction of bombs, and it is conceivable—though much less certain—that extremely powerful bombs of a new type may thus be constructed. A single bomb of this type, carried by boat and exploded in a port, might very well destroy the whole port together with some of the surrounding territory. However, such bombs might very well prove to be too heavy for transportation by air.

In view of this situation you may think it desirable to have some permanent contact maintained between the Administration and the group of physicists working on chain reactions in America.[4]

The letter was given to the president in October 1939 by Alexander Sachs, who was a friend of President Roosevelt. It was timely. Germany had invaded Poland just a month earlier, and that same month the Briggs Committee was appointed to look into the creation of an atomic bomb.

However, it seemed the committee lacked a sense of urgency. Their inaction caused Einstein, Szilárd, and Sachs to write to the president in March 1940, reminding him of the German progress in uranium research. Then in April of that year, a special letter from Einstein, written on his behalf by Szilárd, pressed the chairman of the Briggs Committee on the necessity for "greater speed."[5]

Despite this, research on the project was slow going, as the invention of the bomb seemed remote, and it wasn't until the British submitted a progress report to the Americans in October 1941 that the pace was accelerated. The British report informed the United States that an atomic bomb could be a very real threat by late 1943.[6]

Although some history experts believe that the atomic bomb would have been invented without Albert Einstein's involvement, it was his letters that accelerated the project, and without his signature it might not have been ready in time to drop on Japan.

Other than his signature, Einstein's work on the atom bomb was extremely limited; he accomplished it over a two-day period during December 1941. He was asked for his advice on a theoretical problem, but he was excluded from any other atomic bomb–related work. This was because the committee didn't trust

Einstein's ability to keep the project a secret. The committee's leader said, "I am not at all sure . . . [Einstein] would not discuss it in a way that it should not be discussed."[7]

As the project became a reality, Einstein was able to see beyond, and that in the future the atom bomb would bring with it sobering issues. He wrote in December 1944, "When the war is over, then there will be in all countries a pursuit of secret war preparations with technological means which will lead inevitably to preventative wars and to destruction even more terrible than the present destruction of life."[8]

Although the bombing of Japan was in 1945, Einstein withheld any public statement about it until 1946. The *New York Times* stated: "Prof. Albert Einstein . . . said that he was sure that President Roosevelt would have forbidden the atomic bombing of Hiroshima had he been alive and that it was probably carried out to end the Pacific war before Russia could participate."[9] He later wrote, "I have always condemned the use of the atomic bomb against Japan."[10]

In November 1954, just five months before his death, Einstein regretfully reminisced: "I made one great mistake in my life . . . when I signed the letter to President Roosevelt recommending that atom bombs be made; but there was some justification—the danger that the Germans would make them."[11]

· 11 ·

SCIENCE FORUMS

Science without religion is lame, religion
without science is blind.[1]

—Albert Einstein

N 2010, a secular organization known as sci-
enceforums.net interviewed me regarding
my beliefs about Intelligent Design and
other questions relating to faith in God. Their questions were very thoughtful and probing, and revealed

the difficulty many people of science, much like Einstein himself, have with issues of faith. These questions, and my responses, follow:[2]

> **Q**: You've published dozens of books and pamphlets over the years, and you made news recently by distributing an edition of *On the Origin of Species*[3] with your own Special Introduction included—and this is just one of several books in your recent publications that attacks evolution specifically. Why did you feel the need to shift to taking on evolution? What brought about this shift?

> **A**: This isn't a new subject for me. There isn't a "shift." I wrote a book back in 1990 called God Doesn't Believe in Atheists, which, among other things, dealt with the subject of evolution. However, I have written more on the subject recently to answer those who think that the theory of evolution is scientific, and in doing so throw out Intelligent Design.

In 2009, I read *On the Origin of Species* (a very dry read), and came to the conclusion that if Darwin were alive today, he would be snapped up by Disney as an Imagineer. His imagination was incredibly fertile. He lived in a fantasy world. There is nothing real or scientific about his theory. There were no species-to-species transitional forms in his day to confirm his beliefs, either in the fossil record or in the existing animal kingdom, and 150 years later there are still no species-to-species transitional forms. Believers who post at Atheist Central usually fly off the handle when I say that, mistakenly thinking that I am saying that "there are no transitional forms."

However, I maintain that there are no undisputed *species-to-species* transitional forms. No kind of animal has ever evolved into another *kind* of animal. There are transitions within kinds, but, as the Bible clearly says over and over, every animal brings forth after its *own* kind. The missing link is still missing. The theory of evolution is just a belief. Yet millions embrace it as gospel truth because they unquestioningly believe what they have been told by others who, like Darwin, have a fertile imagination. Charles Darwin brought forth after his own kind. Again, there was no "shift," just an increase in my writing on the subject.

> **Q:** The publication of a new edition of *On the Origin of Species* was a controversial one. Before its publication, were you worried about potential negative press, or did you believe it would be well received? And how would you characterize the reception since—positive or negative?
>
> **A:** I wasn't at all worried about negative press. Anything about Intelligent Design is going to get negative press in contemporary media. If by "press" you are also referring to online reaction,

I was surprised by the intensity of opposition.
So-called freethinkers called for censorship.
Atheists posted vicious video clips, one getting
well over a million views. I have always believed
that the free exchange of ideas is very healthy.
Evolution should be discussed. But, as Charles
Darwin said in his foreword to On the Origin of
Species, the opposing side should also be presented. Otherwise you will be left with narrow-
minded, intolerant, and unreasonable people who
have been brainwashed into thinking that there
are no other perspectives. That's what we found.

There are only two perspectives in the issue of
human origins. Either we believe (as does Richard
Dawkins and many others) that nothing created everything, which is a scientific impossibility, or we believe
that something created everything. In Darwin's book
The Ancestor's Tale the professor said, " . . . *the fact
that life evolved out of nearly nothing,* some 10 billion years after the universe evolved literally out of
nothing—is a fact so staggering that I would be mad
to attempt words to do it justice"[4] [italics added]. Atheists are offended by the thought and try to redefine
the definition of "nothing" to save face. But it can't be
redefined. Nothing means nothing. It is nothing, and it
can produce nothing. There is nothing more to say on
the subject, and for the committed atheist, the alternative is unthinkable, in the truest sense of the word.

When we gave 170,000 copies of *On the Origin of Species* away to 170,000 university students in 100 of the top US universities, and 26,000 to university students in Australia and New Zealand, they were very well received. Most people are reasonable. It's only a vocal fringe that are intolerant and call for censorship. It has always been my contention that if I am an "idiot," "a flat-earther," and "an ignorant fool" as Richard Dawkins has publicly said I am,[5] then he should encourage students to read my ignorant foolishness to strengthen his case. Instead, he encourages students to rip out the 52-page foreword I wrote. I wonder why.

Q: Have you achieved your goals with the edition's publication?

A: My goal has never been hidden. It is simply to present the case for Christianity—which is either true or it isn't. My confidence is that it can be proven to be true but putting John 14:21 into practice. I don't want to censor people from learning about the theory of evolution. However, when someone comes to know God, the issue of atheism is closed, and with that comes a trust in the authenticity of His Word—the Bible. It supernaturally follows, and so by default evolution is proven to be just another of the many myths as to the origin of mankind.

Q: What do you make of Christians who nevertheless believe in evolution, such as the famous biologist Theodosius Dobzhansky? He specifically wrote, "I am a creationist *and* an evolutionist. Evolution is God's, or Nature's method of creation."[6]

A: True, Theodosius Dobzhansky believed in God. It's hard not to in the face of this amazing creation. After all, the most intelligent of us can't create a grain of sand, a frog, a bird, or the simplest flower, from nothing. We don't know how to do it. So how intellectually dishonest is it to say that there was no intelligent and eternal Creator? So one doesn't have to be a rocket scientist to believe in the existence of God. All we need is good old common sense, and that's what Professor Dobzhansky had—common sense, and there are plenty of other intelligent people who believe in evolution and in God's existence.

However, those who believe in God and evolution have to throw out Holy Scripture, because the Bible tells us that God created male and female in every kind of animal, and then He gave them the ability to reproduce after their own kind (see Genesis 1). We are told in Scripture that there is one kind of flesh of men, and one kind of flesh of beasts. So the god of evolution and the God of the Bible are incompatible. Evolution didn't "create" anything. It doesn't have any genesis, and its explanation as to why there are male and female within every animal is ridiculously nebulous.

Those who choose to believe in any other god are guilty of violation of the first and second of the Ten Commandments—something called "idolatry"—making a god in our own imagination, and that was the professor's problem.

> **Q:** For this to be a proper interview, it seems like I have to ask a direct question about evolution, so I may as well. It turns out that retroviruses insert their genomes into DNA, and these sequences have been identified—some have been pulled out and turned back into retroviruses in the lab. However, it turns out that humans and other related animals share similar retroviruses, in similar locations in the genome—but not, say, humans and dogs, or other animals not thought to be related to humans. If this is not evidence for common ancestry, what is it?

> **A:** The idea that retroviruses in similar locations in the genomes of different animals and humans prove common ancestry is a logical fallacy of affirming the consequent. The fallacious belief is as follows: If humans and animals share a common ancestor, then we should observe shared retroviruses in their genomes. Shared retroviruses are observed between humans and animals. Therefore, humans and animals share a common ancestor. However, the conclusion of a common ancestor is not the only one possible, so shared retroviruses cannot be used to prove common ancestry. Another possible conclusion

is that humans and animals share retroviruses because they were created by the same Creator, who used similar designs in humans and animals. We share many similarities with most of the creatures on our planet, seen [both] with the microscope and with the human eye. Similarities simply confirm that God made animals and human beings with the same blueprint—with legs, a mouth, a tongue, eyes, ears, a heart, blood, liver, kidneys, lungs, teeth, and a brain, just to name a few.

Q: Now, rather than going on for ages about evolution, I'd actually like to ask some other questions for a moment. Right now, I'm enrolled in a philosophy of religion course, and we're discussing Christian theology and so on. Do you ascribe your views to any particular theology, or do you develop your views independently?

A: My theological views are shaped solely by the Bible. However, I wasn't converted by the Bible. Early Christians didn't have a Bible. The New Testament wasn't even compiled. There was no such thing as the printing press, and most couldn't read. They heard a message, acted upon it, and were converted by the power of God. That was my experience. When I understood the standard of God, that "whoever looks upon a woman to lust after her has committed adultery already with her in his heart," I had a revelation of my own sinfulness. I rightly surmised that if God was just, I was heading for hell, and it was then that I truly understood why Jesus suffered and died on the cross—to take my punishment upon Himself so that I could be pronounced not guilty. I repented and put my trust in the Savior and came to know God. When I then picked up a Bible, it perfectly described my experience. It told me precisely what had happened to me. This ancient "Bronze Age"[7] Book proved itself to be the supernatural Word of the Creator. I have been reading it daily for more than thirty-eight years, and haven't found even one mistake. There are plenty of seeming contradictions, but with a little study, they are easily answered. So, unlike an atheist, I have a foundation for what I believe. I have a clear agenda. I have the unspeakable comfort of a Book filled with immutable promises of God. That Book gives me absolute assurance that what I experienced more than thirty-eight years ago was the power of God in the life of a guilty sinner. Millions, if not billions, have had the same experience, from all walks of life, and from all ethnicities. So my theology isn't an independent or narrow, exclusive, sectarian belief. It is mainstream belief in the universality of God's "Whosever will may come . . ." [a paraphrase of Revelation 22:17].

Q: You've talked about the theory of evolution being like a cloud—it changes constantly as new evidence is uncovered. Isn't it also true that the basic tenets of Christianity have changed over the past two millennia as views about the Bible and Jesus' preaching changed? (For example, the question of whether Jesus was divine was

unsettled until several hundred years after his
death—some argued that He was wholly human;
others argued that He was not human at all and
His suffering was merely an illusion.)

A: When you say, "For example, the question
of whether Jesus was divine was unsettled until
several hundred years after his death—some
argued that He was wholly human; others argued
that He was not human at all and His suffering
was merely an illusion," how do you know that?
How do you know that is true? Isn't it because
you believe history books? You have no way of
substantiation.

There is no question, nor has there ever been
a question, as to the divinity of Jesus for those who
believe Scripture. For example: "In beginning was
the Word, and the Word was with God, and the Word
was God. The same was in the beginning with God. All
things were made by him; and without him was not any
thing made that was made . . . And the Word was made
flesh, and dwelt among us, (and we beheld his glory,
the glory as of the only begotten of the Father,) full of
grace and truth" (John 1:1–3, 14 [KJV]). Or, "Without
controversy great is the mystery of godliness: God
was manifest in the flesh, justified in the Spirit, seen
of angels, preached to the Gentiles, believed on in the
world, received up into glory" (1 Timothy 3:16 [KJV]).
Notice the words "without controversy." These are

only two verses of many that speak of Jesus being the Creator, manifest in human form.

To say that Jesus of Nazareth was merely a man leaves us with a dilemma that He was unquestionably a con man or a madman. If He was just a man, He suffered from the ultimate delusions of grandeur. He believed and said again and again that He was God in human form. He spoke of His preexistence, His power over death, that all humanity would be resurrected from their graves at the sound of His voice, that He was the very source of life itself, that those who ate of His flesh (spiritual, not literal—as some believe) would live forever. He said that if we thirsted, we were to come to Him and drink, that He was exclusively the only way to God and eternal life.

If he was a madman, then we have to attribute such incredible, wonderful, and wise words spoken in the Sermon on the Mount to someone else. Insane people don't say the things He said. Who, then, said them? If it wasn't Jesus, then we should fall at the feet of whoever it was and call him "Lord."

My challenge to those who profess to be open to truth is to humbly read—without presuppositions—Matthew chapters 5–7, and objectively look at the words of the Savior. Or read the Gospel of John. You will no doubt conclude (along with the temple guards the Pharisees sent to arrest Him) that "never a man spoke like this Man" [John 7:46, paraphrased].

Q: Do you feel that science has become a social or moral movement rather than the honest quest for knowledge it is claimed to be? If so, is this a bad thing?

A: I think that science has been forced to become a social movement at times in history. The scientific community should have spoken out when the Roman Catholic Church arrested Galileo. When religion hinders the progress of true science, scientists must lift a voice, or knowledge will be hindered by small minds. This is no doubt why so many evolutionists are so outspoken. They think Intelligent Design hinders the progress of science. However, evolution is not science. There is nothing scientific about it. The two should only be in the same sentence when one is referring to science fiction. So it's a good thing when true scientists speak out publicly, as did Einstein, when so many German scientists turned their honorable profession into a means of killing human beings.

Q: On a similar note, many Renaissance thinkers believed that the role of science was to explore God's creation, while perhaps many modern-day scientists leave out the "God" in that proposition. What do you believe the proper role of science is, in light of your religious beliefs?

A: True, many famous scientists believed in the existence of God: Copernicus, Bacon, Kepler, Galileo Galilei, Newton, Boyle, Faraday, Einstein (who didn't believe in a personal God, nevertheless Einstein called God "Him" and "He")—[these] weren't fly-by-nights. These were brilliant men who saw no contradiction or anything intellectually demeaning about believing that that which was made had a Maker. In fact, to believe the alternative is intellectual suicide. Nonlife cannot produce life.

So I agree with Albert Einstein when he said, "Science without religion is lame. Religion without science is blind," and I'm confident that he was referring to an intellectual belief in God's existence when he used the word "religion," rather than a reference to the established, traditional church. Any scientist who denies that we live in a "creation" or that nature has been "made" or "built" isn't a scientist, in the truest sense of the word. The redefining of these words to fit one's philosophy shows the desperate measures needed to believe atheism. To leave God out of science ("knowledge") is to leave the "wet" out of water. It is nonsensical, or to quote Einstein, "lame."

Q: Imagine, for a moment, a world where religion never existed, for whatever reason. Its citizens go about their lives having never heard of any religion. In your mind, what would the world be like: worse? better? Why?

A: I think that a world without religion would
be a much better world. Imagine no 9/11. Imagine
no terror threats from Islam. No suicide bombs.
Imagine no pedophile priests or money-hungry
televangelists. Imagine no Roman Catholic
Crusades against innocent people or torturous
Inquisitions against those who denied their religion. Imagine no religious nuts carrying signs
at soldiers' funerals, saying that it's good that
they died, or that "God hates fags." Imagine no
religious hypocrisy, and no trail of human blood
down through history through the mass of religious wars. No witch burnings, no hindrances to
science . . . imagine.

Man has always used religion for his own political
or economic gain. Hitler did it. America does it. Iran
does it. The Pharisees in the time of Christ did it.

Religion is a very grimy and murky bathwater,
and those who don't look carefully can easily miss the
baby. A world without religion . . . how wonderful that
would be. May God hasten the day.

SKEPTICS' DIFFICULTIES
WITH A PERSONAL GOD AND
MORAL ACCOUNTABILITY

The most beautiful emotion we can experience
is the mysterious. It is the fundamental emotion
that stands at the cradle of all true art and science. He to whom this emotion is a stranger, who
can no longer wonder and stand rapt in awe, is as
good as dead, a snuffed-out candle. To sense that
behind anything that can be experienced there is
something that our minds cannot grasp, whose
beauty and sublimity reaches us only indirectly:
this is religiousness. In this sense, and in this
sense only, I am a devoutly religious man.[1]

—Albert Einstein

N THIS CHAPTER and the ones to
follow, I will address questions and comments I have received from skeptics (who
have written to me), who, like Einstein, doubt the
validity of the Bible and are offended at the thought

of a personal God. I will also address questions of morality, some of which were asked by readers who were seeking honest answers.

Q. Albert Einstein, a German Jew Scientist that didn't believe in the Biblical God. Adolf Hitler, a Christian (obviously false convert) German Dictator that killed Jews, homosexuals, mentally ill, etc. If Hitler repented for his sins and truly believed in Jesus, he gets in to your Heaven? And good ol' Albert that didn't accept Jesus goes to hell?[2]

A. I'm sure if you and I had been there when two thieves mocked Jesus of Nazareth and blasphemed Him as they hung on crosses, we would have walked away and said that neither of them believed in Jesus. But if you read the biblical account, one of them had a radical change of mind in the face of his death. Something he saw or heard on that cross changed his thoughts on who Jesus was, to a point of turning to his fellow thief and rebuking him for his foolish talk.

He then turned to Jesus and whispered, "Lord, remember me when You come into Your kingdom" (Luke 23:42 NKJV). He was nailed to a cross. He couldn't go anywhere or do anything about his impending fate. He had nothing to lose and everything to gain when he turned to Jesus. And he was saved in a heartbeat from eternal death—hell—by the grace of God.

> Who are you to say that Albert Einstein didn't have that same last-minute experience? Perhaps during the final moments of his life this German Jew turned to the Nazarene Jew who hung on a cross for guilty sinners. Maybe he whispered, "Lord, remember me when You come into Your kingdom." God only knows.

"Jeffrey," another blogger, said, "I tend to think there was never a time when there was nothing, that our universe had a beginning in time, that the cause of that beginning is unknown and probably unknowable, but that there is no particular reason to believe it possessed intelligence and purpose (i.e., that it was God)."[3]

My response to that is, if someone doesn't *know* what caused the universe, he is not an atheist. He may hold onto the label, but in truth he is "agnostic." According to Merriam-Webster.com, the origin of the word *agnostic* is "Greek *agnōstos* unknown, unknowable, from *a-* + *gnōstos* known, from *gignōskein* to know—more at KNOW." The dictionary defines *agnostic* as "a person who holds the view that any ultimate reality (as God) is unknown and probably unknowable."[4] "Jeffrey" said he believes "that the cause of that beginning is unknown and probably unknowable, but that there is no particular reason to believe it possessed intelligence and purpose (i.e., that it was God)." So, he is not an atheist. He is an agnostic, and he therefore cannot speak on behalf of the true atheists, who, like Richard Dawkins, believe that nothing created everything. Dawkins is a true atheist, and his belief is unscientific. Agnostics plead ignorance. They simply don't know.

That which is designed must have a Designer. So if you feel as Jeffrey does, please keep an open mind when it comes to God. Closed and ignorant minds tend to become prisons to those who have them.

"I keep on being told that God knows everything," wrote another skeptic, "that He hears everything, and here you go telling me there are some times He is deaf? That's not what I call omniscience, Ray. Do you?"[5]

If you share this person's skepticism, then I'd have to say that if you are not conscious of the reality of God, it's because you are only two-thirds a person. Each of us is made up of a body (the machine in which one lives), a soul (the real person, that lives within his or her body—the emotions, the will, consciousness, etc.), and the spirit. Your spirit is your "God-conscious" part, and that part of you, if you have not accepted Christ, is "dead in trespasses and sin" (see Ephesians 2:1 NKJV). The plug is pulled, and so you have no light.

It's interesting that this particular inquirer should ask if God is deaf. Eight hundred years before

Christ, Isaiah addressed his question: "Behold, the LORD's hand is not shortened, that it cannot save; nor His ear heavy, that it cannot hear," he wrote. "But your iniquities have separated you from your God; and your sins have hidden His face from you, so that He will not hear" (Isaiah 59:1–2 NKJV).

If you, like this blogger, have not accepted Christ, then you are cut off from God by your sins—yet, the moment you genuinely repent and trust the Savior, you will come out of the darkness into the light (see 2 Corinthians 4:6). But if you stay proud and rebellious, you will carry on without being conscious of His existence, and when and if you do pray in that spirit, your prayers won't get past the ceiling. You have God's Word on it (see Psalm 66:18).

> **Q.** What about people who are unable to make that decision? Where would my 18 month old daughter go? How about my 3 year old niece, or her 7 year old sister? How about a severely mentally handicapped adult? Or an aborted fetus? I once worked with a guy who had been a devout Christian but stopped believing in God after receiving a serious brain injury. It also left him prone to seizures and with severe brain damage. In his case, it was not a choice to turn from God, but a result of severe trauma. Heaven or Hell?[6]
>
> **A.** The religious leaders at the time of Christ also had an interesting question. They asked

> Jesus about a woman who had been married to seven different men. Each man she married died, one after the other. Their question was, "Whose wife will she be in Heaven?" Jesus replied that they asked that question because they didn't know the Scriptures, nor did they understand the "power" of God. (See Matthew 22:25–29.)

Those who ask this same question have the same problem. They don't know the Scriptures, nor do they understand the power of God. When it comes to the Scriptures, the skeptic stands on his own oxygen hose. He doesn't believe that they are the Word of God, and they are of no benefit to those who refuse to believe. This is no different from any other documents in life. If you are told that you have been left money in a will and you don't believe the will is authentic, you won't bother to claim your inheritance. Your beliefs will govern your actions.

Regarding the "power" of God, I have often pointed out that the god the atheist doesn't believe in, doesn't exist. He conceives of a god in his own mind, and then dismisses his own creation. Making any god in your own image is a form of idolatry and is a violation of the second of the Ten Commandments.

I have a problem describing the power of God because He is indescribable. But let me try with something to which anyone may be able to relate—my dog.

Without exaggeration, he has at least five hundred *thousand* hairs on his small, furry frame. A quick study will show that every piece of his soft fur is growing in a different direction. It was preprogrammed to do so. What sort of mind could create every growing hair on his body? What sort of power can create a living animal that can think, reproduce its own kind, reveal his emotions through his eyes, have instincts to eat, drink, chase cats, be loyal, and protect property?

Then think of all the different types of dogs in the world, all the other animals, all the people, the insects, fish and birds, all with instincts, emotions, desires, eyes (at least most of them) that can see, and brains that can think. These are all just a tiny part of the incredible creation of an almighty and indescribable God. He made them and gave them life. He can see everywhere at one time, He knows everything, and with Him nothing is impossible.

All that to say, God has the power and will to do that which is right on Judgment Day. With all our professed intelligence, we don't know how to make a tiny seed from nothing. The eternal God made *every-thing* from nothing; therefore the distance between man's impotence and God's infinite power solves the "Don't Understand How" (DUH) problem.

Another writer sniped, "According to your doctrine, Hitler is in heaven. He was a Christian creationist, like you. If you're going to heaven because you believe in God, so did he."[7] My response:

Believing in God or being a creationist has nothing to do with going to Heaven. Every sane person believes in the existence of God. I believed in God before I was a Christian. Going to Heaven comes by the grace of God (His mercy) through trust in Jesus.

Our beliefs have nothing to do with reality. If I didn't believe in gravity, atoms, radio waves, the wind, love, etc., because I have never seen any of these things, does not mean they don't exist because I don't believe in them. Their existence has nothing to do with what I believe or don't believe.

To say that Hitler was a Christian because he believed in God reveals not only your lack of understanding as to the nature of Christianity, but also of history. Hitler killed off pastors and put Nazis in their place. He was responsible for the murder of millions which reveals that he didn't have the evidence that comes with being a Christian—the foremost being love.

Q. "If I am lusting," wrote "Froggie,"[8] "is that caused by a demon?"

A. It would be nice to be able to blame a demon for our sins, but that's not the case. The Bible says, "But every man is tempted, when he is drawn away of his *own* lust, and enticed. Then when lust has conceived, it brings forth sin: and sin, when it is finished, brings forth death" (James 1:14–15, italics added).

So we are drawn away by our own lust and then "enticed." However, if you give yourself to lust, you will almost certainly become possessed with an unclean spirit (a demon) and you will find yourself consumed with perverted sexual thoughts. It is then that you will become a slave to sin (see John 8:34). Without the mercy of God intervening, it is a ball and chain that will drag you into Hell.

You will be like a man who boasts that he has no problem with cigarettes, and he doesn't—while he gives himself to the consumption of two packs a day. But it's when he tries to stop, he finds that he is a slave to the deathly habit. Study these verses on the subject of an unclean spirit: Matthew 12:43, Mark 1:23–26, Mark 5:2, Mark 7:25, Luke 9:42, Luke 11:24.

Q. An atheist wrote: "I have no sin. I've made some poor choices and some bad judgments over the years, but we make amends where we can and move on . . . realize many of you need this emotional crutch to cope, and that's OK. Otherwise you'd be out killing people and such." A Christian, responding to the atheist, had this to say: "What is your objection to killing people? If it's just a 'poor choice' or a 'bad judgment' what's the problem? Murderers can just make amends where they can, and move on . . ."

A. The issue here is morality. If the Creator is without morals, we are all okay. That means that there is no accountability. That means there's no right or wrong. Rape, murder, adultery, Nazi Germany, etc., are nothing but poor choices and bad judgments. But why would any rational person seriously entertain such a philosophy? The wisdom of Solomon has the answer. Scripture says, "Because sentence against an evil work is not executed speedily, therefore the heart of the sons of men is fully set in them to do evil" (Ecclesiastes 8:11).

Why is it that we give ourselves to things that we know are wrong? It's because God doesn't respond. If a man rapes a woman and successfully silences her by threatening to take her life if she snitches, there's no swift divine justice. The man got away with evil. When humanity gives itself to pornography, fornication, adultery, blasphemy, etc., there is no response from Heaven. God is silent when it comes to evil. So the erroneous conclusion is that God doesn't exist, or at least He doesn't care or hear.

There is one other conclusion. It's the one we see (in principle) with civil law. When a criminal who gets away with murder becomes emboldened in his crime, it doesn't mean that civil law doesn't care about what he's doing. It means that he is making things worse for himself when the law catches up with him.

The same applies to humanity every time we violate God's Law (the Ten Commandments). The Amplified Bible puts it this way (this translation takes the original Greek and brings out the depth and meaning of each word):

"And do you think or imagine, O man, when you judge and condemn those who practice such things and yet do them yourself, that you will escape God's judgment and elude His sentence and adverse verdict? Or are you [so blind as to] trifle with and presume upon and despise and underestimate the wealth of His kindness and forbearance and long-suffering patience? Are you unmindful or actually ignorant [of the fact] that God's kindness is intended to lead you to repent (to change your mind and inner man to accept God's will)? But by your callous stubbornness and impenitence of heart you are storing up wrath and indignation for yourself on the day of wrath and indignation, when God's righteous judgment (just doom) will be revealed. For He will render to every man according to his works [justly, as his deeds deserve] . . . " (Romans 2:4–6).

No one is getting away with a thing. God's justice will be swift, severe, and very thorough:

"But I say unto you, that every idle word that

men shall speak, they shall give account thereof in the day of judgment. Time will prove that to be true" (Matthew 12:36).[9]

Q. Ray, I have a serious question that I am not sure how to answer when asked. When I talk to teens and tell them that if they lust after a woman/man, they've committed adultery in their heart, I've had some tell me, "I'm not married, so how can I commit adultery when adultery is sex between a married person and someone other than their spouse." How do I answer that?[10]

A. There are certain things that we human beings define as being morally wrong. One of them is adultery. No sane person would try to justify adultery as being morally okay. For those who are not sure as to what adultery is, according to any dictionary it is having sex with someone who is married. The definition traces itself back to the seventh of the Ten Commandments, and under Israel's civil law, anyone who violated that commandment was subject to capital punishment.

The moral law and the consequences of violating it give us a glimpse of how serious adultery is in the sight of God. So how serious is the sin of lust in God's eyes? It's as serious as the act of committing adultery. Whoever looks upon a woman to lust for her has committed adultery already with her in his heart.

So in God's Book, lust *is* adultery . . . no matter what the dictionary or society says. See Matthew 5:27–28 for details.

Q. It seems much more likely that a number of small changes over the course of millions of years led to the complexity we see today. If not, how do you explain things like the blind spot in the human eye? The fact that our urinary tract runs through the prostate? The tail all embryos have and some babies are born with? The fact that we breathe and eat through the same hole? None of those make sense in light of special creation, but they do make sense when you actually understand the processes of evolution.

A. I must point out the language of speculation that you are forced to use in your opening sentence. Words like "seems" and "likely" are always present when a Darwinian believer speaks of what he believes. Let's address your issues. I don't have a blind spot in my eye. Both of them see very well and I am thankful for the 137 million light sensitive cells that make sight possible. Do you have a blind spot in your eye? If you do, I suggest that you see an optician and see if he can either fix it, or get you another eye.

You may detect a little sarcasm, which I think is thoroughly justified. To think that a camera lens could create itself is insane, but to believe that the human eyes, and the eyes in 1.4 million different species created themselves, is off the charts.

The prostate wraps around the tube that carries urine out of your bladder. If you think evolution caused the prostate to wrap around the tube, and you think it's a poor design, then you have a problem with the designing mind of evolution.

As far as I know, all mammal embryos have "tails." The embryo has to end somewhere. Leaves have tail endings, dogs have tails, and Darwin had the biggest tale of all, and you believed him, so now you think we came from fish. But the ending of the embryo isn't vestigial, and neither is the "tail" bone in human beings. Without it you wouldn't be able to go to the bathroom each day because the muscles that make it possible would have nothing with which to connect.

Finally, to breathing. The next time you have a bad cold and your nose is really stuffed up, take a moment to thank God that He gave you another opening that allows you to breathe. Then use that opening to confess your sins, forsake them, and then trust in the Savior so that you will be forgiven on the Day of Judgment.[11]

Q. Is there free will in Heaven? If there is free will in Heaven is it possible to sin in Heaven? If the answer to either of those questions is no then clearly either free will is not as important as you make out OR it is possible for God to give people free will AND remove the ability for them to sin. God can apparently do anything. So why could he not have created beings that had both free will and lacked the ability to sin?

A. Most Christians believe that God allowed the Fall because He didn't want to make us as "robots." He therefore gave us a free will, and that entailed the freedom to choose right and wrong. That explanation has never satisfied me. This is because it is (hopefully) evident that in Heaven, God isn't going to give the vast sea of redeemed humanity the ability to sin. That didn't work with just one couple, so it's not going to work with innumerable multitudes. So we will clearly live in a state where we aren't robots but we won't have the capability to sin. That makes sense.

The question then arises as to why God didn't do that with Adam and Eve. Why did He create them with the freedom of choice, and therefore allow them to bring all this misery, death, and an impending Hell upon the entire human race?

That's the first of two questions that I will humbly and with due reverence ask when I get to Heaven.

The second is, "Why does God allow children to suffer?" I'm not talking about suffering the pain of a broken leg or some sort of temporal disease. I'm talking about excruciating pain from a disease that sucks out their life, leaving them as a skeleton, and then taking them terrified to an untimely grave. If He is loving and kind, why doesn't He heal them? He has the power to do so. Nothing is impossible for God. So why not heal them? The atheist therefore concludes that God is either a tyrant or He doesn't exist.

Here's why I am still a Christian despite my unanswered questions. I know that the sun exists. I also know that it is directly responsible for the agonizing deaths of many innocent people. Deserts are littered with the dry bones of those who found themselves under its terrible burning heat. I know that there are holes in this analogy because the sun isn't a thinking, rational part of God's creation, but my point is, do I then conclude that the sun doesn't exist because it killed these people?

I can't deny the reality of the existence of God simply because I have unanswered questions. I know He exists because of the axiom of creation. I know He exists because I know Him experientially, and have an all-consuming love for Him that embraces all of my heart, mind, soul and strength. I'm not angered, worried, frustrated, concerned or upset by these questions, because I love and trust Him. I know that the time will come when I find out the answers, and I don't mind waiting.[12]

Q.   People ask me How can you believe in a Bible that is full of heroes who do horrible things? One person wrote: "Lust, greed, lies, blasphemy, theft," one person quipped. "All of these things can be found in the Bible and then some. Gotta love that old time religion!"

A.   The Bible has a whole lot more than lust, greed, lies, blasphemy, and theft in its many pages. It's full of adultery, murder, rape, jealousy, pride, incest, [hatred], homosexuality, fornication, and torture, just to name a few.

Perhaps you are not aware that the Scriptures mainly relate the history of the Hebrew nation. It begins with the creation of the first male and female and their tragic fall from fellowship with their Creator. This didn't come because of the eating of an apple [as many believe]. It came through the sin of disobedience [see Romans 5:19]. Then Scripture traces the same rebellion as it manifested itself in the whole human race. The Bible doesn't hide the sinful heart of man. It exposes each man's wickedness and warns that God has appointed a day in which He will judge the world in righteousness. So whatever you do, don't make the mistake of writing off the Bible as being evil, when it simply exposes evil. Has it exposed the evil in your heart yet, or aren't you aware of it?

The amazing thing about this collection of 66 books is that their common thread (through the Old Testament) is God's promise to release mankind from his greatest enemy—death itself. The New Testament tells us how He did it. See John 3:17–18 for details.[13]

Q. "How did the 16,000 or so kinds on Noah's ark become the 1.4 million species today?"[14]

A. I wouldn't let it worry you too much. It won't be an issue on Judgment Day. Just say to yourself, "With God, nothing is impossible," or as the cynic says, "Goddidit." That solves the issue. It also solves the issue of how Jesus fed 5,000 people with five loaves and two fish, how He walked on water, calmed a storm by speaking to it, etc.

But if you do like to ask difficult questions, ask an atheist how the 1.4 species came from nothing. Despite his protests, that's what he believes. When he says that he doesn't know how everything began, ask him how is it that each of the 1.4 species evolved both male and female— how they reproduced before that time, and why females evolved anyway, if things were buzzing along with just males.

Press him on the issue. Make him think about what he believes. Then ask him if he can make a bird from nothing. When he says that nobody can, call him on his intellectual dishonesty in his belief that nothing made everything.

Believing all the strange things in the Bible is a breeze, compared to the fantasies the average atheist believes.

Q. One angry individual wrote in, saying, "If I get hit by a bus when I go to buy some more cigarettes and I stand face to face with God I'll tell him exactly what I think of him. As Woody Allen said, 'God has some explaining to do.'"

A. Most of us won't die under the wheels of a bus. We tend to see them coming. What we don't see coming is an aneurysm in our sleep, or being rear-ended by a truck, or liver cancer, or a massive heart attack. Death has a way of sneaking up on us, but one thing is sure, it *will* come.

When the atheist stands before God, it will be a waste of time telling Him what he thinks of Him. God *already* knows what we think. He sees the thought-life and hears every word spoken. He knows the enmity that human beings have towards Him, and He has even gone to the trouble of telling us exactly why we feel enmity towards Him.

"Enmity" is a state of hostility. Here's the explanation from Romans 8:7, from the *Amplified Bible*. This version of the Scriptures (as the name suggests), amplifies the English, by going back to each Greek word and opening up its meaning:

[That is] because the mind of the flesh [with its carnal thoughts and purposes] is hostile to God, for it does not submit itself to God's Law; indeed it cannot."

Our godless thought-process is called the "mind of the flesh." The "flesh" is the biblical way of expressing the fact that we get pleasure out of sin. The flesh loves gluttony, pornography, violence, adultery, sexual fantasies, etc. We delight in that which is wrong. If you disagree, then explain why it is that almost every movie, television program, magazine, and newspaper is filled with stories of sex and violence? *Of course* we love these things, and it's the love of them that makes us despise the very thought of God and His moral Law. We are like criminals who despise the police, because they uphold civil law.

Woody Allen may be big with words, but he is little on delivery. He is a sad man who is fearful of dying. And that fear of death will plague him until he takes the time to listen to the explanation that God has *already* given us in His Word.

Allen once lamented, "I don't want to achieve immortality through my work . . . I want to achieve it through not dying." The offer of not dying is there, and we ignore it at our own peril. Listen to the warning of Scripture: "How shall we escape, if we neglect so great salvation . . . [?]" (Hebrews 2:3).[15]

How indeed?

· *13* ·

SKEPTICS' DIFFICULTIES
WITH THE BIBLE AND
INTELLIGENT DESIGN

Many take to science out of a joyful sense of
superior intellectual power; . . . others are
to be found in the temple who have offered
the products of their brains on this altar for
purely utilitarian purposes. Were an angel
of the Lord to come and drive all the people
belonging to these two categories out of the
temple, the assemblage would be seriously
depleted, but there would still be some men,
of both present and past times, left inside.[1]

—Albert Einstein

I CAN UNDERSTAND WHY SO many
have difficulty when it comes to some parts
of the Bible. There are stories about Noah,
Moses, Joshua, etc., that are harder to swallow than
Jonah's whale. Plus it contains teachings that aren't

just contrary to the way of this world; they are deeply offensive to it. Take for instance the Bible's continual admonition to teach children the "fear of the Lord." Most think that any fear is bad, let alone teaching children to fear. However, upon closer examination the fear of the Lord makes sense.

I once dropped a cable for my iPhone onto the floor while driving my car. I was immediately tempted to pick it up, but I didn't because of something I saw when I was nine years old. It was a "short" before the main movie in a theater, showing a happy family being driven in their car by their beloved dad.

When something dropped onto the vehicle's floor, he bent down for a split second to pick it up, hit a concrete wall on a country bridge, and killed his entire family. That clip left an indelible mark on my small mind and has stopped me from risking my life a number of times.

Skeptics don't want to fear the Lord. The god of their own making (or no god at all) is much more attractive, so they hold onto the idea that the world was made by chance and that there is no one to hold them accountable. You should never be afraid to teach the fear of the Lord to your children. The world will scream foul, but you will instill in your child something that will preserve him, not only in this life but in the one to come.

The fear of the Lord will keep him from lying, stealing, fornicating, and hating. It will protect him from murder, adultery, drunkenness, drug abuse, and getting sexually transmitted diseases. It will free him from guilt, selfishness, greed, envy, jealousy, anger, homosexuality, pornography, and 101 other self-destructive sins. But most of all, if the fear of the Lord will drive him to the foot of a bloodstrained cross, it's there that he will find everlasting life.

However, the fear of God is only one of many biblical doctrines that are contrary to what the Bible calls "the carnal mind." And it's the carnal mind that drives many to search the Scriptures to find other "offenses" that do nothing but build a bigger barrier between them and God. May He help us to knock those barriers down.

Someone once wrote to me and said, "Dear Ray, please address some of the rebuttals that have been thrown at you. Such [as]: Your idea of evolution (one species giving birth to another) would disprove evolution. The Bible being written by man. The Bible being horribly inconsistent. Your God doing immoral acts in the Bible. Why atheists 'don't exist,' but you still address us as such? Providing support that your God is the actual Creator (as opposed to other religions).

Why the Bible condemns people for genetic defects (i.e., Dwarfs)." Here's how I responded:

> Species-to-species evolution is not one species "giving birth" to another. It is the theory that human beings evolved from primates (that they are our common ancestor). There is no empirical evidence for any species evolving from another species—either in the fossil record and in the existing creation. Every animal brings forth after its own kind. All a believer in evolution has is a belief that what he has been told is true.
>
> The Scriptures were written by men, but they were "inspired by God" (see 2 Timothy 3:16). Do you write a letter or does your pen? You do the writing, and the pen is the instrument you use. In the Bible, God used man to pen His letter to humanity.
>
> The Bible is not "horribly inconsistent." It's not even slightly inconsistent. The problem is that it is not "rightly divided" by many of its readers. One great key to understanding Scripture is the correct place of Law and grace. Failure to do that will leave any reader in confusion.
>
> God has never done anything that is immoral. All of His judgments are righteous and true altogether. He has proclaimed the death sentence upon the whole of humanity, and if He carried out swift justice today and treated each of us according to our sins, we would be in Hell in a second.

But He is rich in mercy and is waiting for sinners to repent (this is referred to as the Day of Grace). So it would be wise to draw back your holier-than-thou finger, and not stand in judgment over Almighty God.

It is impossible for any atheist to exist—because to say that there is no God, you need absolute knowledge. No one has that but God. That's why Richard Dawkins uses the word *probably* when he says that there is no God. He doesn't know if God doesn't exist, so he (like every other professing atheist) is actually agnostic. It is because of this that I often use the word *professing* before the word atheist, but it becomes tiresome to do so every time.

It is easy to provide evidence that the God of the Bible "is the actual Creator (as opposed to other religions)." Ask Him yourself. He promises to reveal Himself to all who come on His terms (see John 14:21). No religion claims that. To them, the Creator is unknowable.

So there's the gauntlet. But most won't take up the challenge because they "love the darkness and hate the light. Neither will they come to the light, lest their deeds be exposed" (See also John 8:31, 21).

Finally, the Bible does not condemn people for genetic defects. Those who believe that it does would probably think that the Scriptures are horribly inconsistent—because they don't "rightly divide" them.

The Old Testament (Law) carries hundreds of "typologies" of the New Testament (grace).

You can see an example in John chapter 3:14–15: "And as Moses lifted up the serpent in the wilderness, even so must the Son of Man be lifted up, that whoever believes in Him should not perish but have eternal life." The opening of the Red Sea, the life of Joseph, the conquering of Jericho, etc., are all hidden types of New Testament truth.

Your reference is presumably to those with physical deformities not being allowed to minister in the Temple of God (under the Law). This is a type (a foreshadowing) of the perfection that is required for those who enter the Kingdom of God (under grace).

Without the perfect righteousness of the Savior, none of us could enter Heaven.[2]

***

Evolution is an important social issue because it shapes the worldview. Those who believe it embrace it as a hill upon which to die, because it opens the door to the endless pleasures of fornication, adultery, homosexuality, and pornography with no moral responsibility. If we are mere primates, then anything goes. If God created us and we are morally responsible as the Bible maintains, then that throws an ice-cold wet blanket on those pleasures. So the war against creation is just that—a war. It has nothing to do with truth. It's all to do with winning the war to hold onto (and to get more) pleasure. That's why when we deal with someone who believes in evolution, we deal with someone who is unreasonable in the truest sense of the word. He will come at you with a list of questions that, to him, fortify his worldview. These are questions that are evidence that the Bible is filled with errors and conclusively prove that it is just the word of man and not the Word of God. Take for instance the argument that the Bible lists bats as being birds:

> These you shall have in abomination among the birds; they shall not be eaten, for they are detestable: the eagle, the ossifrage, the ospray, the kite, the whole species of falcon, every kind of raven, the ostrich, the nighthawk, the sea gull, every species of hawk, the owl, the cormorant, the ibis, the swan, the pelican, the vulture, the stork, all kinds of heron, the hoopoe, and the bat (Leviticus 11:13-19 AMP).

Rather than seek after truth, evolutionists conclude that the Bible is wrong. "Bats are not birds; they are mammals," they might say. For them the argument is over. But the answer is simple. There was not a Linnaean classification when these verses were written. The scientific classification for the bat didn't exist. Neither was there one for a bird. The classifications for animals used to be determined by their function or their form. In those days a bird simply meant the "owner of a wing." It comes from a Hebrew word meaning "to cover or to fly." Tell that explanation to someone who believes in evolution, and they usually run back to their list and give you another rabbit trail to run down. (And with the Internet and atheist sites there are plenty that fortify their belief in evolution.)

For the last two hundred years Darwinian evolution has been a volatile issue, but in recent years it has exploded across the earth. There's a good reason for this. When I was a youth and wanted to get my sinful eyes onto a lusty picture, it wasn't easy to do. I remember once having a friend buy a newspaper that had a scantily dressed woman on the back page. That was all I could get. But since the emergence of the Internet, any youth can get instant hard-core pornography in seconds. This generation has been able to give itself to darkness like no other, and the consequence is that it's a generation that hates the light.

Over a hundred years ago, Charles Spurgeon had the insight to see how potentially evil Darwin's theory was. In a sermon he called "Hideous Discovery," preached back on July 25, 1886, he said of Darwinian evolution:

> In its bearing upon religion this vain notion is, however, no theme for mirth, for it is not only deceptive, but it threatens to be mischievous in a high degree. There is not a hair of truth upon this dog from its head to its tail, but it rends and tears the simple ones. In all its bearing upon scriptural truth, the evolution theory is in direct opposition to it. If God's Word be true, evolution is a lie. I will not mince the matter: this is not the time for soft speaking.[3]

Little did Spurgeon know that this "hideous discovery," (this "survival of the fittest") would inspire the Nazi Holocaust. Few realize that Hitler was a big fan of Darwin and how his ideas fanned the killing of millions. Having studied Darwin, I am sure that he would have also been horrified had he foreseen what would take place in the future because of his ideas. I'm sure that he didn't foresee that his theory would convince millions that man is merely an animal—that he's not made in the image of God, and that that worldview would produce such a disregard for human life that it would pave the way for the horror of abortion.

The problem in fighting Darwinian evolution is that those who embrace it have no moral ethic. They can lie (and do lie) to strengthen their position—and why not? If there's no God and no Judgment Day, then no one is morally accountable, and the Ten Commandments are irrelevant. The end (pleasures) justifies the means (lying). So any person who believes in creationism is vilified and painted as a knuckle-dragging, anti-science, homophobic, woman-hating, slave-loving, anti-choice bigot whose agenda in life is to brainwash children with a fairytale that delights in telling people that they are going to hell.

But if that is how they want to paint us, so be it. Whatever the case, we must still speak the truth in love. And that I will do.

Here are three important points about evolution.

1. It rests on faith.

2. It is not scientific.

3. It is just a symptom, not the cause.

FAITH IN THE THEORY

If there's one word that evolutionists and atheists hate, it's the word *faith*. They will do linguistic cartwheels to distance themselves from it, insisting that they don't have faith. They have science. They don't *believe*. They *know*. They distance themselves because faith has close ties to God. However, do a little probing and you will find that Darwinian evolution rests on nothing but faith.

Ask a believer in evolution if he *believes* in evolution, and you will find that he does. He *trusts* that the information given to him is correct, and he *relies* on it. He trusts, relies, has faith in what he has been told by those who he *believes* are experts. He either believes it or he doesn't believe it. He either has faith or he doesn't have faith. In reality, he can't distance himself from it.

THE SCIENCE OF DARWINIAN EVOLUTION

The word *science* simply means "knowledge." To find out if something is scientific it has to pass the scientific method, which means it must be observable and repeatable. However, Darwinian evolution is unobservable.

Most evolutionists are confused as to what they believe. They think that adaptation and Darwinian evolution are one and the same thing. They are not. Adaptation is a change within a species. Dogs adapt. They change. So do cats. You can have small dogs, such as the terrier, and big dogs, such as great Danes. Both are dogs. They are within the canine kind.

You have the cat and the tiger. Both are cats. They are the feline kind. That's not Darwinian evolution. We see adaptation all the time—in lizards, bacteria, fish, etc.

Darwin believed that sometime in the future there would emerge proof for a change of kind (he called them "families"). He hoped that we would see one kind evolving, in time, into another kind. But there is no evidence for any such thing. Ask any evolutionist this question: Darwin spoke of a change of kinds—not speciation or adaptation, but a change of kinds. Using the scientific method (it must be observable and repeatable), can you give me one example of a change of kinds?

They can't do it, because there isn't one. If you don't believe it, check out a movie I produced called *Evolution vs. God.*[4] I took a camera to UCLA and USC and asked evolutionary scientists that exact question, and all four professors floundered like fish on the sands of the Sahara desert. They couldn't answer because there wasn't an answer. Darwinian evolution is unproved and unprovable. How can we observe and test something that supposedly happened sixty million years ago?

Creationism, on the other hand, is both observable and testable. It is founded on the account given to us in Genesis chapter 1:

And the earth brought forth grass, the herb that yields seed according to its kind, and the tree that yields fruit, whose seed is in itself according to its kind. And God saw that it was good. So the evening and the morning were the third day . . . So God created great sea creatures and every living thing that moves, with which the waters abounded, according to their kind, and every winged bird according to its kind. And God saw that it was good. And God blessed them, saying, "Be fruitful and multiply, and fill the waters in the seas, and let birds multiply on the earth." So the evening and the morning were the fifth day. Then God said, "Let the earth bring forth the living creature according to its kind: cattle and creeping thing and beast of the earth, each according to its kind"; and it was so. And God made the beast of the earth according to its kind, cattle according to its kind, and everything that creeps on the earth according to its kind. And God saw that it was good" (Genesis 1:12-13, 22-25, NKJV).

Notice the liberal use of the word *kind*. We see that in the existing creation. Nothing changes kind. Elephants have elephants, giraffes have giraffes, horses have horses, chickens have chickens, fish have fish, etc. Nothing changes kind. We see the same thing in the fossil record. Those who believe that they have evidence in the fossil record merely have bones that they *believe* to be old because they have *faith* in fallible dating processes. Darwinian evolution rests on nothing but blind faith. It's not scientific because it doesn't and can't pass the scientific method. Creationism doesn't rest on faith. You can see (observe) the unchanging kinds in creation and in the fossil record.

EVOLUTION IS THE SYMPTOM

As a Christian, my agenda isn't to convince people that God exists. They already know that. God has given light to every man. It isn't to talk people out of believing in evolution and into believing Genesis chapter one. They don't want to be talked out of it. It would be easier to floss the back teeth of hungry lions at the Los Angeles Zoo at feeding time than to get them to let go of their beloved sins. Besides, people can end up in hell believing in God and Genesis. Eternal salvation comes through repentance and faith in Jesus, and not a mere intellectual acknowledgement that God exists and that Genesis is true.

My agenda is to preach the gospel to them, have them experience the miracle, life-changing supernatural experience of the new birth of John chapter 3. That deals with evolution and atheism in an instant. When I was converted to Jesus Christ back in 1972, in a moment of time I became a believer in Genesis. I also became pro-life and pro-"one man and one woman in marriage." I became anti-adultery, anti-fornication, anti-lying, anti-stealing, anti-blasphemy. I instantly loved what God loved and hated what God hated. This is because my Creator had given me a new heart with new desires.

Evolution is a symptom of the disease of sin. It blinds to the truth, and the only thing that can open blind eyes is the glorious gospel of Jesus Christ—something we will continue to look at in future chapters.

THE SEVEN MOST IMPORTANT QUESTIONS YOU WILL EVER BE ASKED

The highest principles for our aspirations and judgments are given to us in the Jewish-Christian religious tradition. It is a very high goal which, with our weak powers, we can reach only very inadequately, but which gives a sure foundation to our aspirations and valuations. If one were to take that goal out of its religious form and look merely at its purely human side, one might state it perhaps thus: free and responsible development of the individual, so that he may place his powers freely and gladly in the service of all mankind . . . It is only to the individual that a soul is given. And the high destiny of the individual is to serve rather than to rule, or to impose himself in any other way.[1]

—Albert Einstein

*E*INSTEIN SPOKE MUCH ABOUT LIFE and about the existence of God. If there is no God, life has no purpose. We are nothing but accidents, speeding through space at sixty-three thousand miles an hour on a huge ball of dirt. No one knows how we got here, no one knows why, and no one knows where we are going. Conversely, if there is a God, then life has a purpose. It has meaning. It means we were created by God and that there is Someone ultimately in charge.

So in this chapter, we will look at this vital issue in depth through the answers to seven important questions.

1. HOW DO WE KNOW GOD EXISTS?

It's amazing how many people think that God's existence is a matter of "faith." They think that we choose to accept that an invisible God exists, without any real evidence for His existence, and we just "believe."

Could you believe that a soldier's barracks had no builder? Obviously someone put it together, because buildings don't happen by themselves. The fact that the building exists is positive proof that there was a builder. Who could believe that a building—with its doors, windows, heating, air-conditioning, carpet, electricity, etc., happened by accident, made from nothing?

Its *design* adds to evidence of a designer. For example, the door is made for people to walk through. It has a handle and hinges. Windows are made for us to see through. The air-conditioning keeps us cool in summer, and the heating keeps us warm in winter. The lighting helps us see when it's dark, and the carpet is for our added comfort. The building was *intended* specifically for our use.

In the same way, creation is proof that there was a Creator. Keep in mind that we can't create anything from nothing. We don't know how to begin. If you disagree, then make me a seed—from nothing. Make it living, so that it grows into a plant that produces an edible fruit, and make it with the ability to create more seeds within the fruit, so that you can plant them and make more plants and more fruit. So if we can't even make one seed, how intellectually deceitful is it for any rational human being to believe that nothing created everything?

But there is more. The evidence shows that this earth upon which we live was *intended* for our use. We have lighting during the day so we can see what we are doing. The sea breeze keeps the air fresh and cool, and the warmth of a massive ball of fire in the sky keeps us warm and dry. Cows give us succulent meat to eat and leather to wear. They chew grass and give us milk, and from the milk we get cream, cheese, butter, yogurt, and ice cream. Sheep also give us mouthwatering meat to eat, and wool from their backs can be made into warm sweaters for our comfort. Chickens lay eggs for us to scramble, and sacrificially provide finger-lickin' food on our plates.

We have oceans that are rich with tasty fish for our dinner; the soil yields juicy fruits for the table and a huge variety of vegetables to keep us healthy. Trees breathe out oxygen for us to breathe in, and we breathe out carbon dioxide for them to breathe in.

We have eyes to enjoy the beauty of this amazing creation, ears to listen to melodious music and to hear the songs of a myriad of beautiful birds that usher in the morning light. We have a mass of taste buds to relish mashed potatoes and gravy.

Add to this the wonder of man being made for woman and woman for man, and the fact that dogs give us enjoyment and keep us company. We have brilliant, white snow on which to ski, massive waves on which to surf, the joys of blue skies, green grass, and white beaches with amazing and crystal-clear water.

On top of all this, gravity keeps our feet firmly grounded so we don't spin off into space, as this massive ball of dirt upon which we live spins around at breathtaking speed.

The amazing design all around us screams of the unspeakable genius of an incredible Designer. No wonder the Bible calls the professing atheist a "fool" (Psalm 14:1).

Look at Albert Einstein's "Everything Is a Miracle":

> There are only two ways to live your life. One is as though nothing is a miracle. The other is as though everything is a miracle.
>
> But without deeper reflection one knows from daily life that one exists for other people; first of all for those upon whose smiles and well-being our own happiness is wholly dependent, and then for the many, unknown to us, to whose destinies we are bound by the ties of sympathy.
>
> A hundred times every day I remind myself that my inner and outer life are based on the labors of other men, living and dead, and that I must exert myself in order to give in the same measure as I have received and am still receiving.
>
> A human being is part of a whole, called by us the "Universe," a part limited in time and space. He experiences himself, his thoughts and feelings, as something separated from the rest—a kind of optical delusion of his consciousness. This delusion is a kind of prison for us, restricting us to our personal desires and to affection for a few persons nearest us.

> Our task must be to free ourselves from this prison by widening our circles of compassion to embrace all living creatures and the whole of nature in its beauty.

> Only a life lived for others is worth living.[2]

So there is no question as to whether or not God exists; which brings us to the second question.

2. WHAT DOES GOD HAVE THAT I NEED?

So here is our problem. We are *all* going to die. God is not. He is eternal. If I want to live forever, I have to somehow find a bridge to this eternal Creator. This is why so many billions have been interested in religion, down through the ages. This is why I became intensely interested in the subject of God on the night of my conversion. For about twenty years I didn't give God serious thought for a minute. I was like a man who, understandably, didn't have any thought about a particular cure until he understood that he had the terminal disease that the cure treated. That's a huge revelation for any human being to have.

Almost all religions have the common knowledge that God requires us to do that which is right, and we have done wrong. Consequently, the core of all the major religions is that they must *do something* to "justify" themselves. The four-year-old tries to *justify* why he hit his sister—"*She* hit me first!" His explanation is an attempt to exonerate himself of guilt. He is seeking what is called "justification." And the thought behind those who are religious is, *If I can somehow justify myself by doing things and* earn *God's favor, perhaps He will let me live.*

Religious deeds are often combined with self-suffering as a means of seeking God's mercy—*If He is angry at me for my sins, maybe I can pay for them myself in this life.* The toddler admits that he hit his sister, so he punches himself in the chest as a form of punishment. This is the motive for self-mutilation, fasting, self-denial, lying on beds of nails, sitting on hard pews, and so forth. People believe God *needs* these acts so they can be justified before Him.

However, biblical Christianity teaches that no one can justify himself in the sight of God. There is a good reason for that, which brings us to the next important question.

3. WHAT IS GOD LIKE?

To a child, the sun may look like just a bright, not-too-big ball in the sky, but it's actually a huge mass of burning hydrogen and helium that's 1,392,000,000 miles in diameter and 333,000 times the mass of the earth. If I believed that it were square, made of ice, and that it came out at night, my belief wouldn't change the sun's reality. It is what it is, despite my beliefs.

In the same way, it doesn't matter what we believe about the nature of God. He is what He is, despite our beliefs. So if we are going to consider His attributes, we must let go of every preconceived and erroneous image we have and look at what He reveals about Himself in His Word, the Bible.

We are told that God is a "spirit" (John 4:24). That means He is invisible to the natural eye. We believe in many things that are invisible: atoms, radio waves, television waves, love, history, and the wind, just to name a few. The life that inhabits our bodies is unseen. When we die, that invisible life leaves the shells in which we live. God is the wellspring of that unseen life.

Perhaps the most important thing we should know about God is that He is holy (Exodus 15:11). Isaiah 57:15 says, "For thus says the One who is high and lifted up, who inhabits eternity, whose name is Holy: 'I dwell in the high and holy place, and also with him who is of a contrite and lowly spirit, to revive the spirit of the lowly, and to revive the heart of the contrite'" (ESV). He is absolute moral perfection, and because of His moral perfection, His very nature demands supreme justice. To put it in human terms, He is like a good judge who uncompromisingly upholds justice. He *always* does that which is right and just.

If a judge doesn't do what is right, if he turns a blind eye to serious crimes, he's not a good judge. He is corrupt, and should therefore be brought to justice himself.

It is because God is good that He has set aside a day in which He will judge the world in righteousness (Judgment Day). That will be the day when every murderer gets exactly what is coming to him. He will also punish thieves, liars, rapists, fornicators, adulterers, murderers, and blasphemers. Please stay with me now, because we are going to look at a biblical truth that changes everything.

Would you consider yourself to be a good person? Most of us do. So let's have a quick court-martial and see if you are (as you maintain) a morally good person. You will be put on the stand, and I will cross-examine you. All I ask of you is that you tell the truth, the whole truth, and nothing but the truth, so help you God. Can you manage that? Here goes.

How many lies have you told in your life? Have you ever stolen anything? Have you ever used God's name in vain? Jesus said, "Whoever looks at a woman to lust for her has already committed adultery with her in his heart" (Matthew 5:28 NKJV). If you have lied, stolen, used God's name in vain, or looked with lust, then you are a lying, thieving, blasphemous adulterer at heart, and that's only four of the Ten Commandments.

The dictionary says that a *murderer* is "a person who commits murder." But the Bible goes further. It says that if you *hate* someone, you are a murderer (1 John 3:15). Of course, the person who has hated someone hasn't necessarily *physically* committed murder, but in God's eyes he or she has done the deed, because the *intent* is there and He therefore considers that person guilty of murder (see Hebrews 4:12). That's how high God's moral standards are, and that will be the standard on Judgment Day (see Romans 2:12). So, have you ever hated anyone?

The Tenth Commandment says, "You shall not covet" (Exodus 20:17 ESV). To covet means "to have an inordinate or wrongful desire."[3] Covetousness is a sin of the heart. We violate the Tenth Commandment simply by having an unlawful desire.

When Jesus spoke on the subject of lust (which is a form of covetousness), He spoke of it sexually, and said that when we lust we violate the seventh commandment, which says, "You shall not commit adultery" (Exodus 20:14 ESV). The dictionary definition of *adultery* is "voluntary sexual intercourse between a married person and someone other than his or her lawful spouse."[4] But Jesus said that when we lust after someone (when we covet him or her sexually), we commit adultery in the heart. Again, the person hasn't *physically* committed adultery, but in God's morally perfect eyes the desire is the same as the deed. The dictionary confines adultery to a married person. The Bible broadens it to include *anyone* who looks with lust, whether that individual is married or unmarried. If you have looked with lust, then you have committed adultery in your heart, and that's the standard God will judge with on the Day of Judgment. If you've got red blood in your veins and a working conscience, you will know that you are in big trouble for transgressing that commandment. So what are you going to do to try and "justify" yourself?

Here's what changes everything. Before you try to justify yourself, keep in mind that God is a perfect Judge. In His eyes you are a wicked criminal. You are guilty of violating His Law (the Ten Commandments). I can't overemphasize the importance of your grasping this—your understanding of the fact that you are a devious criminal will almost certainly determine your eternal destiny. Here is why. It is because we are wicked criminals in God's eyes that *any good works or self-sacrifice on our part are, in truth, detestable attempts to bribe the Judge of the universe.* The Scriptures warn that the sacrifice of the wicked is an abomination to the Lord (see Proverbs 21:27). There is absolutely nothing we can do to justify ourselves in God's sight.

How, then, do you plead? Innocent or guilty? You can't say you are innocent, because you are not. You dare not point to your "good" works, because you haven't any, and look what happens to the guilty on Judgment Day: "Do you not know that the unrighteous will not inherit the kingdom of God? Do not be deceived. Neither fornicators, nor idolaters, nor adulterers, nor homosexuals, nor sodomites, nor thieves, nor covetous, nor drunkards, nor revilers, nor extortioners will inherit the kingdom of God" (1 Corinthians 6:9–10 NKJV).

God's wrath abides on you because of your sin (see John 3:36). The Bible says that you are an enemy of God in your mind because of wicked works. If you die in your sins and He gives you justice, you will damned in hell (see Revelation 21:8). What should you do? You have only one option. It is to throw yourself on the mercy of the Judge. That brings us to the next question.

4. WHAT HAS GOD DONE FOR THIS SINFUL AND DYING WORLD?

The Bible compares us to lost sheep. We have "gone astray; we have turned, every one, to his own way." We have gone astray and live with our backs to God, but we are then told "and the LORD has laid on Him the iniquity of us all" (Isaiah 53:6 NKJV). What does that mean?

When I was about eight, I thought nothing of throwing a stone the full length of our street, just to see how far it would go. My problem was that I didn't understand that sometimes actions can have serious consequences.

One day I was in a tree-filled empty lot, three doors down from our house. For some reason I threw a stone into the trees. Suddenly I heard the sound of glass breaking, and high-tailed it out of there like a rabbit that had just seen a hungry fox.

A few minutes later, the fox was at our back door. Then I heard my mom call my name, and then ask, "Did you just throw a stone through Mr. Prescott's window?" I stepped out of my room and said that I had. I can't remember anything else about the incident except that my mom has said a number of times how proud she was that I had done the right thing by telling the truth.

When it comes to the issue of sin, we don't understand that there are deadly, serious consequences. We lie, steal, lust, covet, and blaspheme without too much thought. It's no big deal. But every time we do so, we smash the window of God's Law, and that Law demands retribution. Now He's waiting for us to do the right thing and fess up. If we refuse to come out in the open, we will pay for it ourselves, and there will be hell to pay.

So what are you going to do? We have already seen that you can't justify yourself. Simply do the right thing. Confess your sins to God. He knows all about the broken window, and in His great mercy He has already paid for a new one Himself.

God became a Man in the person of Jesus of Nazareth—a morally perfect Man; then He offered Himself as a sacrifice for the sin of the world. When Jesus was on the cross, the Father laid on Him the sin of us all.

Think of it this way again. God is a Judge. We are guilty criminals who have violated His Law. Jesus stepped into the courtroom and paid the fine for us. That means, because of the suffering death and resurrection of Jesus Christ, God can *legally* dismiss our case. He can commute our death sentence and allow us to live! Can you understand that? He took the bullet so you don't have to:

THE SEVEN MOST IMPORTANT QUESTIONS

> For God so loved the world that He gave His
> only begotten Son, that whoever believes in Him
> should not perish but have everlasting life. For
> God did not send His Son into the world to con-
> demn the world, but that the world through Him
> might be saved. He who believes in Him is not
> condemned; but he who does not believe is con-
> demned already, because he has not believed in
> the name of the only begotten Son of God. And
> this is the condemnation, that the light has come
> into the world, and men loved darkness rather
> than light, because their deeds were evil. (John
> 3:16–19 NKJV)

Do you remember how man-made religions seek
justification? Look at what God did through the
Savior: "[He] was delivered for our offences, and was
raised again for our justification." (Romans 4:25 KJV).

This is what makes Christianity unique among
other religions. Instead of man seeking justification,
in Christ God justifies the guilty sinner. Everlasting
life is a free gift of God, and that brings us to a very
important question.

5. HOW DO I APPROACH HIM TO GET
THE GIFT?

If I want to speak to a five-star general, I have to
go to him on his terms. The importance of his rank
demands it. When you and I come to God, we have

to come on His terms, and His stipulation is that we approach Him through humility and *faith*. This isn't an intellectual faith that He exists. When the Bible speaks of "faith" in God, it is referring to a *trust* in Him. There's a huge difference between the two.

Trust is the basis for many things we do in life. We trust bankers with our money. We trust historians to give us the truth about history, our doctors to prescribe us the right medicine, and teachers to offer us correct information for our education. We trust that our dentist knows what he's doing when he drills a tooth, and our mechanic when he fixes our brakes. For a soldier, trust is walking in front of a buddy who has a fixed bayonet, or letting someone you hardly know pack your backup parachute.[5]

The 1.5 billion people who travel by air annually trust more than pilots when they fly in a plane. Without too much thought, they trust their precious lives to unseen pilots, unseen air traffic controllers, and aircraft mechanics they will never see or meet.

Trust is the glue that cements friendships. It's what holds a marriage together. If trust goes out the door, so does the relationship. If you don't trust someone, it means you think that person is not worthy of your trust. He or she is devious. Think of how you would feel if you said, "I love my mother. She is so faithful. She sure keeps her promises," and someone responded with, "I don't trust her!" His lack of trust would hopefully anger you, because it would be insulting to your mom. Insulting another human being by a lack of faith is bad enough, so whatever you do, don't insult God through a lack of faith in Him, because "without faith it is impossible to please Him: for he that comes to God must believe that He is, and that He is a rewarder of those who diligently seek Him" (Hebrews 11:6 kjv).

So with genuine sorrow ("contrition") confess your sins to God, turn from them ("repentance") and trust alone in Jesus Christ as your Savior and your Lord. The moment you do that, God will "justify" you and grant you everlasting life. "Therefore being justified by faith, we have peace with God through our Lord Jesus Christ" (Romans 5:1 nkjv).

Even though God is holy and we are sinful, upon God-given repentance and faith in Jesus we can have fellowship with Him, because He is rich in mercy to all who call upon Him.

If you have never repented of your sins, pray something like this today, because you may not have tomorrow:

> Dear God, I have sinned against you by violating your Law. Please forgive me. If you were to judge my many sins, I would justly end up in hell. But because you are rich in mercy and have provided a Savior, I can be forgiven through the death and resurrection of Jesus Christ. I surrender my life to Him and trust Him alone for my salvation. In His name I pray. Amen.

6. IS THE BIBLE RELIABLE?

The early Christians didn't have a "Bible," as we know it. The New Testament wasn't compiled. There was no such thing as the printing press. Few could read. Their salvation wasn't dependent upon owning or even believing the Bible, but upon their relationship with the person of Jesus Christ (see 1 John 5:11–13). They heard a *spoken* message, believed it, put their trust in the living risen Jesus, and were converted by the power of the unseen God. (See 1 Thessalonians 1:5.)

That was in the first century AD. In 1972, I had a similar experience. After I was converted, I picked up a Bible and it confirmed my experience. I was experiencing a peace that I couldn't understand, and I felt clean on the inside. It was as though I was a completely new person. I had a sudden love for God and couldn't stop thinking about Jesus and what He had done on the cross. I was amazed to read in Scripture about a "peace that surpasses all understanding" (Philippians 4:7 NKJV), that if any man is in Christ he is a "new creature" (2 Corinthians 5:17 KJV), that the love of God has been "shed abroad in our hearts" (Romans 5:5 KJV), and that the Holy Spirit points the believer to Jesus. Again, *the Bible* didn't convert me; it simply confirmed my experience and became an instruction book for me to know God's will.

The New Testament was written in Greek, which is a far more complex language than English. The Amplified Bible expounds the original language so that we can understand its true meaning. Here is a key promise from Jesus, translated directly from the Greek: "The person who has My commands and keeps them is the one who [really] loves Me; and whoever [really] loves Me will be loved by My Father, and I [too] will love him and will show (reveal, manifest) Myself to him. [I will let Myself be clearly seen by him and make Myself real to him]" (John 14:21).

Believe the Scriptures, and make a habit of reading them every day without fail (see Psalm 1 for the benefits of a disciplined life). As you obey what you read, Jesus will become very real to you.

When someone tells you the Bible isn't reliable—that he thinks he has found a mistake—look into it closely and you will find *he* is the one who has made the mistake.

Another evidence for the divine inspiration of the Bible is its amazing prophecies. We can hardly predict tomorrow's weather accurately (many a picnic has been rained upon because of misguided faith in human forecasters), but the Scriptures perfectly predicted the time in which we live, written thousands of years ago. Do you know the signs of the end of this age? Here are some of them:

1. The Scriptures tell us that there would be money-hungry Bible teachers who would slur the Christian faith and deceive many: "...there will be false teachers among you ... and many will follow their destructive ways, because of whom the way of truth will be blasphemed. By covetousness they will exploit you with deceptive words..." (2 Peter 2:1–3).

2. There would be wars, earthquakes, famines, and widespread disease: "For nation will rise against nation, and kingdom against kingdom. And there will be famines, pestilences, and earthquakes in various places" (Matthew 24:7).

3. The moon would become blood red: "The sun shall be turned into darkness, and the moon into blood, before the coming of the great and awesome day of the Lord" (Acts 2:20).

4. People would become selfish, materialistic, and blasphemous: "...in the last days perilous times will come: for men will be lovers of themselves, lovers of money, boasters, proud, blasphemers..." (2 Timothy 3:1, 2).

5. People would forsake the moral Law (the Ten Commandments): " . . . because lawlessness will abound, the love of many will grow cold" (Matthew 24:12).

6. Religious hypocrisy would be prevalent: "For [although] they hold a form of piety (true religion), they deny and reject and are strangers to the power of it [their conduct belies the genuineness of their profession]" (2 Timothy 3:5, AMP).

7. Men would deny that God created the heavens, and that He destroyed the world through Noah's flood: "There shall come in the last days scoffers . . . for this they willingly are ignorant of, that by the word of God the heavens were of old, and the earth standing out of the water and in the water: whereby the world that then was, being overflowed with water, perished" (2 Peter 3:3, 5, 6).

8. The future would become frightening: " . . . men's hearts failing them from fear and the expectation of those things which are coming on the earth, for the powers of the heavens will be shaken" (Luke 21:26).

9. Skeptics (motivated by the sin of lust) would mock these signs, claiming they have always been around: " . . . scoffers will come in the last days, walking according to their own lusts, and saying, 'Where is the promise of His coming? For since the fathers fell asleep, all things continue as they were from the beginning of creation'" (2 Peter 3:3, 4).

10. The city of Jerusalem is pivotal in Bible prophecy. Scripture says that it would become a major political problem for the nations: "And it shall happen in that day that I will make Jerusalem a very heavy stone for all peoples . . ." (Zechariah 12:3).

The powerful Arab nations want to annihilate the nation of Israel, so that they can have Jerusalem as their center of worship. " . . . Jerusalem shall be trodden down of the Gentiles, until the times of the Gentiles be fulfilled" (Luke 21:24).

Jerusalem was controlled by the Gentiles (non-Jewish nations) until 1967 when the Jews took its possession. For the first time in 2,000 years, the Jews stepped into Jerusalem. This sign shows us where we are on the prophetic clock. We are living on the very edge of the coming of God's kingdom—when His will, will be done on earth, as it is in Heaven. The tragedy, however, is that despite these evident signs, most will ignore the warning to get right with God.

7. HOW CAN I BE SURE OF MY SALVATION?

The reality of your salvation will be directly in proportion to the authenticity of your repentance. If you fake it, you will certainly have a false conversion and eventually fall away from the faith. That was the experience of Judas Iscariot, and you don't want to follow in his steps.

The false convert (the hypocrite) is like a Christmas tree. He may look healthy and have ornamentation, but because he has no root, in time he will wither and die. But if you are "rooted and grounded" as a Christian (Ephesians 3:17 NKJV), you will grow in time (again, see Psalm 1).

The bottom line will be your attitude to sin. For many people, lust is extremely pleasurable, and therefore probably the most difficult sin from which we turn. The unsaved world is mystified as to why any sane person would deny himself such pleasure. But as a Christian, you know something the world doesn't.

More than likely you love chocolate. You would be crazy to stop eating it—unless your doctor told you that were extremely allergic to it, and that the smallest amount would instantly kill you. Then you would have a good reason to keep it from your lips, despite the pleasure it would bring.

The Bible makes it clear that lust will kill you and then damn you in hell:

> You have heard that it was said to those of old, "You shall not commit adultery." But I say to you that whoever looks at a woman to lust for her has

already committed adultery with her in his heart. If your right eye causes you to sin, pluck it out and cast it from you; for it is more profitable for you that one of your members perish, than for your whole body to be cast into hell. (Matthew 5:27–29 NKJV

When lust has conceived, it brings forth sin: and sin, when it is finished, brings forth death. (James 1:15 NKJV)

So every time lust sweetly calls your name, you have a choice: to play the hypocrite and follow sin to death and hell, or follow righteousness to everlasting life. Remember, any self-denial from sin doesn't *earn* salvation. It's simply evidence that you have truly been converted.

If you are a Christian, God promises that anything life throws at you can only come by His permission. He will allow it because it will benefit you. That doesn't mean that when it rains you won't get wet. Lightning falls on the just and the unjust. It simply means that in the light of eternity, God will work every situation to your good. Christianity doesn't promise a smooth flight. But it does guarantee a safe landing.

In 1413, John Huss was summoned to appear before the Roman church council in Constance. When he was thrown into a prison for nineteen months, awaiting trial for his faith, and then sentenced to death, he no doubt knew from the Scriptures that God would work things out for his good (see Romans 8:28). When he was burned alive at the stake and his charred, lifeless body fell among the ashes, the wonderful promise that God would work out for his good such an unspeakable horror remained unwavering.

On November 9, 2006, "three Christian high school girls were beheaded as a Ramadan 'trophy' by Indonesian militants who conceived the idea after a visit to Philippine jihadists, a court heard. The girls' severed heads were dumped in plastic bags in their village in Indonesia's strife-torn Central Sulawesi province, along with a handwritten note threatening more such attacks. The note read: 'Wanted: 100 more Christian heads, teenaged or adult, male or female; blood shall be answered with blood, soul with soul, head with head.'"[6]

In Malatya, Turkey, April 18, 2007, three Christian men who were working in a Bible publishing office were accosted by Muslims who had only days earlier attended their Christian Easter services. Their hands and feet were bound and they were tortured with butcher knives (for two hours), and finally had their throats cut. Each of the murderers carried a note saying, "We did this for our country. They were attacking our religion."[7]

In each and every case of horrific persecution, those who love God and are called to His purposes can stand on the wonderful assurance that He will work all things out to their good.

In closing, look at how this Christian mother's faith holds her in a fiery trial (she wrote to our ministry about a gospel tract):

> In June my breast cancer became advanced bone cancer and this tract has been an excellent tool to share as I give my testimony in churches or just one on one. I have 6 children so God has given our family a "megaphone" through this cancer diagnosis which is opening many doors to point others to Jesus . . . I am asking permission to make copies of "I Have a Problem" tract to use in upcoming events. I am attending a woman's retreat at the first of February. I will be at the back of the room on a sick bed. This will certainly allow me to briefly interact with many who come my way to pray for me and I for them! Bone cancer is really painful and debilitating. This attracts interest. I do not want to waste my cancer! MY HEART'S DESIRE IS TO POINT OTHERS TO JESUS![8]

So don't trust in Jesus because you are afraid of what tomorrow will bring. Trust in Him because you are a sinner and you need a Savior on the day of judgment. We don't know what tomorrow will bring, but even death itself cannot separate us from Him.

Look at this wonderful promise from the Word of God. Read it purposely, meditate on it thoughtfully, memorize it, and then believe it with all of your heart:

> Who shall separate us from the love of Christ? shall tribulation, or distress, or persecution, or famine, or nakedness, or peril, or sword? As it is written, For your sake we are killed all the day long; we are accounted as sheep for the slaughter. Nay, in all these things we are more than conquerors through him that loved us. For I am persuaded, that neither death, nor life, nor angels, nor principalities, nor powers, nor things present, nor things to come, nor height, nor depth, nor any other creature, shall be able to separate us from the love of God, which is in Christ Jesus our Lord. (Romans 8:35–39 KJ2000)

None of us know what the future holds, but when we trust in the Savior, we know Him who holds the future . . . and there's no greater consolation than that.

· 15 ·

EINSTEIN'S POPULAR
IDOL

My position concerning God is that of an
agnostic. I am convinced that a vivid consciousness of the primary importance of
moral principles for the betterment and
ennoblement of life does not need the idea of
a law-giver, especially a law-giver who works
on the basis of reward and punishment.[1]

—Albert Einstein

S ONE READS the many dif-
ferent thoughts Einstein had
throughout his life, it is easy to
become confused as to his beliefs. At different points in
life he seems to change from a deist to an agnostic, and

then to a pantheist. His beliefs shifted like a puffy cloud on a hot summer's day. However, even though a cloud may change its shape, it is still defined as a "cloud." Its form may alter, but its definition doesn't. As we have already established, Einstein was a classic idolater.

In a high-tech world, little is heard in or out of the church about idolatry, probably because it seems an irrelevant subject to modern man. We don't bow down to idols. However, the word *idol* has many definitions. We have one word for it in English, but it has nineteen words to describe it in the Hebrew language,[2] ranging from a "figure" to a "shape," to a "statue" and stones and molten images.

As we have also seen, if we want to throw ourselves into the joys of sin with abandonment, we must first rid ourselves of any serious thought of being morally accountable to God. This can be easily done through atheism (which is an abandonment of all reason and common sense), or through idolatry.

In a letter to a friend, Mark Twain, the famous American author and humorist, not only shows his contempt for his Creator, but believes that he is morally superior to God: "I am plenty safe enough in his hands; I am not in any danger from that kind of a Deity. The one that I want to keep out of the reach of, is the caricature of him which one finds in the Bible. We (that one and I) could never respect each other, never get along together. I have met his superior a hundred times—in fact I amount to that myself."[3] He was deeply offended by the God of the Bible. He also said:

> If I were to construct a God I would furnish Him with some way and qualities and characteristics which the Present lacks. He would not stoop to ask for any man's compliments, praises, flatteries; and He would be far above exacting them. I would have Him as self-respecting as the better sort of man in these regards.

> He would not be a merchant, a trader. He would not buy these things. He would not sell, or offer to sell, temporary benefits of the joys of eternity for the product called worship. I would have Him as dignified as the better sort of man in this regard.

> He would value no love but the love born of kindnesses conferred; not that born of benevolences contracted for. Repentance in a man's heart for a wrong done would cancel and annul that sin; and no verbal prayers for forgiveness be required or desired or expected of that man.

> In His Bible there would be no Unforgiveable Sin. He would recognize in Himself the Author and Inventor of Sin and Author and Inventor of the Vehicle and Appliances for its commission; and would place the whole responsibility where it would of right belong: upon Himself, the only Sinner.

He would not be a jealous God—a trait so small that even men despise it in each other.

He would not boast.

He would keep private His admirations of Himself; He would regard self-praise as unbecoming the dignity of his position.

He would not have the spirit of vengeance in His heart. Then it would not issue from His lips.

There would not be any hell—except the one we live in from the cradle to the grave.

There would not be any heaven—the kind described in the world's Bibles.

He would spend some of His eternities in trying to forgive Himself for making man unhappy when he could have made him happy with the same effort and he would spend the rest of them in studying astronomy.[4]

Notice how Twain, like Einstein, shapes a god that has no sense of morality, justice, or truth. Instead of holding man accountable for his wickedness, his god would blame himself for evil. Twain put into words his idolatrous imaginations.

The idolater is like a heinous criminal looking at a good judge and imagining him having no sense of right and wrong, that there was no punishment for crime, and that the judge's reason for existence should be for the criminal's happiness, rather than to be vindictive.

Twain also said:

> To trust the God of the Bible is to trust an
> irascible, vindictive, fierce and ever fickle and
> changeful master; to trust the true God is to
> trust a Being who has uttered no promises, but
> whose beneficent, exact, and changeless ordering
> of the machinery of His colossal universe is proof
> that He is at least steadfast to His purposes;
> whose unwritten laws, so far as to affect man,
> being equal and impartial, show that he is just
> and fair; these things, taken together, suggest
> that if he shall ordain us to live hereafter, he will
> be steadfast, just and fair toward us. We shall not
> need to require anything more.[5]

It was Charles Spurgeon who perceptively said
that if you see someone who is anti-God, follow him
home and you will see why. It is easy to see why
Mark Twain was, like Einstein, offended by the God
of the Bible (and therefore his moral accountability
to Him). We don't have to follow him home to see
why. Some of his writings are so sexually explicit I
wouldn't quote them in this book.[6] He even inter-
mingles his sexual thoughts with God, Solomon,
Adam and Eve, prayer, and heaven.[7]

Prominent former atheist Antony Flew, who died
in 2010, also embraced idolatry. He was an outspoken
advocate of atheism, writing thirty-five works for

the nonbelief in God. Flew explained his atheism by saying, "I was not always an atheist. I began life quite religiously. I was raised in a Christian home and attended a private Christian school. In fact, I am the son of a preacher."[8]

However, he couldn't reconcile that God could be loving and all-powerful. He commented, "By the time I reached my fifteenth birthday, I rejected the thesis that the universe was created by an all-good, all-powerful God."[9] Later on in life, he said, "My departure from atheism was not occasioned by any new phenomenon or argument. Over the last two decades, my whole framework of thought has been in a state of migration. This was a consequence of my continuing assessment of the evidence of nature."[10]

However, by 2004, Flew publicly denied that life could have emerged from matter alone. Eventually, he came to insist that the laws of nature could only have come from a divine mind. In other words, there must be a God.

Flew's public announcement in 2004 that he had rejected atheism and now had a belief in God was a philosophical blow to the atheist world. Christians championed his rejection of atheism.

However, Professor Flew never accepted Christianity. He rejected any divine revelation and completely rejected any thought of divine judgment and of hell. He told the *Sunday Telegraph* (London) that the god he had come to believe "probably" existed is "most emphatically not the eternally rewarding and eternally torturing God of either Christianity or Islam," but only God as First Cause of the universe. He also said, "I want to be dead when I am dead and that's an end to it. I don't want an unending life. I don't want anything without end."[11] In other words, he rejected the God who reveals that He is just and holy, and instead (like Einstein) embraced *his own concept* of God.

One of my historical heroes was inventor Thomas Edison. Although he is often touted as an atheist, he was simply an idolater. He said, "I do not believe in the God of the theologians; but that there is a Supreme Intelligence I do not doubt."[12] He believed in God, but a god with whom he felt comfortable.

Most atheists are "reverse" idolaters. They pick out God's harsh judgments from the Old Testament and create a god who is a tyrant, void of any mercy or kindness. Then they say they don't believe in that god and feel righteously justified.

Of course, they shouldn't believe in that god, because their concept of God doesn't exist. It's an idol, a nonexistent figment of their imagination. Such is the predictable way of us sinners.

Yet, atheists often turn the tables and say that the God I worship may also be an idol. True. That's why God gave us the Scriptures—to show us His true nature. It is the God of the Scriptures that man tries to reshape to suit himself, but in doing so he *deceives* himself. Our Creator never changes.

A guy named Jay once wrote and asked me a very good question. "Ray," he said, "could you explain to me what it means to 'know the Lord'? I often hear you ask 'ex-Christians' (in quotes for your benefit) if they 'knew the Lord.' I would like to better understand your relationship with the Lord. How do you communicate with Him? How does He communicate back? In what way can one know that they know the Lord in the same manner as you?"[13]

This is a great question. Let me first explain—to him and to those reading this book—why I use the wording "know the Lord." One who "knows the Lord" is the biblical definition of a Christian. It is used many times in Scripture, but it is particularly used in reference to the gospel. Jeremiah 31:34 says, "And they shall teach no more every man his neighbor, and every man his brother, saying, Know the LORD: for they shall all know me, from the least of them unto the greatest of them, saith the LORD: for I will forgive their iniquity, and I will remember their sin no more" (KJV). Because Jesus took our sin upon Himself, we can be forgiven. That means instead of being separated from God (have no real consciousness of His presence or reality), we can have fellowship with Him. Jesus said, "This is eternal life, that they may know You, the only true God, and Jesus Christ whom You have sent" (John 17:3 NKJV).

I often say there's no such thing as an atheist who is an "ex-Christian." This is because there are only two alternatives that the "ex-Christian" can choose. If he ever knew the Lord, then "the Lord" exists; therefore, there's no such thing as atheism. Or he simply "thought he knew the Lord," then he didn't, and was therefore a false convert (a hypocrite). Some in this category fall away from the faith, but many stay within the church as "goats" among the sheep and will be sorted out on Judgment Day. Notice Scripture's wording in reference to that day: "Not everyone who says to Me, 'Lord, Lord,' shall enter the kingdom of heaven, but he who does the will of My Father in heaven. Many will say to Me in that day, 'Lord, Lord, have we not prophesied in Your name, cast out demons in Your name, and done many wonders in Your name?' And then I will declare to them, '*I never knew you*; depart from Me, you who practice lawlessness!'"

(Matthew 7:21–24 NKJV; emphasis added).

False converts don't "know the Lord," And He "*never* knew" them. There was no intimate relationship with them because they were still in their sins (playing the hypocrite).

Now to the essence of Jay's question. What does it mean to know the Lord? Probably the best way I could relate it to you would be to say that it is very similar to me knowing my wife. We are best friends. She is forever in my thoughts. Even when we are in different locations—say, I am at my home office, and she is at our ministry—our temporary physical separation doesn't change the fact of our relationship. I still know her, love her, and trust her implicitly.

The moment I repented and put my trust in Jesus, I began a relationship with God that is more real than my relationship with my wife. It has the same feelings, but it's not contingent upon those feelings, but rather on trust (as are all relationships). Even though I don't "see" God, as with the relationship with my wife even when we are apart, I still have a relationship with God. The Bible puts it this way: "Without having seen Him, you love Him; though you do not [even] now see Him, you believe in Him and exult and thrill with inexpressible and glorious (triumphant, heavenly) joy. [At the same time] you receive the result (outcome, consummation) of your faith, the salvation of your souls" (1 Peter 1:8–9 AMP).

How do I talk to God? The same way everyone else does. Most nights I get up to pray (around midnight—something I have done since 1982). How does He talk to me? Through the Bible. It's a "lamp to my feet and a light to my path" (see Psalm 119:105 ESV). I have read the Bible every day without fail since my conversion in 1972. I communicate with God through prayer, and He speaks to me through His Word.

Jay's final question was, "In what way can one know that they know the Lord in the same manner as you?" One must simply humble himself, take a tender-conscience look at the Ten Commandments. If you, like Jay, are wondering the same thing, first, be honest with yourself: Have you lied, stolen, blasphemed, looked with lust (adultery of the heart)? Judge yourself—guilty or innocent? Heaven or hell? Then look to the cross—God in the person of Jesus Christ taking your punishment upon Himself, paying the fine so that you can leave the courtroom. Through His death and resurrection, you can have everlasting life—if you will repent (something the hypocrite fails to do) and trust the Savior. If you do these things, you will come to know the Lord (see John 14:21 for details).

One atheist was quite upset that in my personal response to Jay, I compared my relationship with God to my relationship with my wife. Among other things, he wrote:

> I'll first note that the description of knowing the Lord given here is a far cry different from any marriage I've ever witnessed, and certainly nothing like mine. I interact with my wife; I talk to her verbally, and hear her audibly. I embrace her to show my love, and she embraces back. Sometimes we have differing opinions and sometimes this leads to arguments. We often take walks in the evening with our dog, and discuss the day's events. I try to comfort her when she's upset, and she does the same for me. I do trust her implicitly and she is always in my thoughts.

I wrote back, "I don't believe your wife exists. Prove to me that she does. Until then, I think that she is a figment of your imagination."

He then sent me an e-mail containing a picture of him and his wife. When I answered him, I said, "How do I know that's your wife?"

"I will also take a photo of my marriage license if you wish," he replied, and he did.

"I think it's one of those bogus $5 Vegas marriage licenses or something you have done on Photoshop."

"I'll have to require you to make an effort to come meet her . . ."

"You could easily find an actress who could pretend to be your wife."

Finally, he wrote, "I've provided you with as much evidence as is available to me at this moment, and I'm perfectly willing to provide more upon request." To which I responded:

> You have provided me with no evidence at all. I do not believe the woman you say is your wife exists. Therefore, in my mind, she doesn't exist. The truth is, you can't prove to me that she is your wife if I have the presupposition that she doesn't exist, and I'm not open to "reason." Creation is 100 percent proof that there is a Creator *to anyone open to reason.* For some reason, I am surrounded on this blog by unreasonable people—those who aren't open to reason. But I will keep trying to reach you (and others) as long as I have life in me. Thanks for writing. Love to your wife.

WHY I TRUST GOD

> For any one who is pervaded with the
> sense of causal law in all that happens, who
> accepts in real earnest the assumption of
> causality, the idea of a Being who interferes
> with the sequence of events in the world is
> absolutely impossible. Neither the religion
> of fear nor the social-moral religion can
> have any hold on him.[1]
>
> —Albert Einstein

I COULDN'T *NOT* BELIEVE IN the
existence of God, even if I wanted to. Not
only do I have creation as empirical and
axiomatic evidence, but I have the very real evidence
of a changed life, and then the supporting evidence of

a faithful Creator "who interferes with the sequence of events"—One who has had a guiding hand through the years of my life. Let me explain.

I'm from New Zealand. It's a pretty small country of nearly four million people, and something like *50 million* sheep. (Although, they're not sure of the exact number, because the man who counts them keeps falling asleep.)

I was born in 1949, just four years after the Second World War. My Jewish mom married a Gentile (to the horror of her parents), and Mom and Dad decided to put "Methodist" on my birth certificate, because they were concerned that there may be another Nazi-type holocaust. Despite the Methodist label, in my twenty-two years as a non-Christian, I was left without any real instruction about God.

I started surfing at the age of thirteen, graduated high school at seventeen, and started working at a bank. During that time I met and fell in love with a beautiful girl named Sue. She was made for Comfort—a very cute four feet, eleven inches tall.

Around that time I saw a picture of a professional surfer I admired, wearing a fringed cowboy jacket, so I made one for myself. My friends so liked it that they asked me to make jackets for them. There was so much interest that I left the bank, opened a combined leather gear and surf wear store, and eventually made fifteen hundred jackets.[2]

One warm Saturday afternoon, Sue was visiting our house. I was eighteen, and we were yet to be engaged. To my delight, she was making dinner for our family, but it wouldn't be ready for an hour or so. I had just purchased a new surfboard and decided to walk across to the beach and catch a few waves before dinner.

I called my dog and headed for the beach. The animal was crazy, but went crazier whenever I mentioned the beach. He ran around in circles of joy. Chasing seagulls meant as much to him as riding waves meant to me.

As we walked along the sidewalk, the joyous thought of chasing terrified gulls must have overtaken him. He ran ahead of me toward the beach. I called, "Jordie, come back!" No response. I called again as he ran across the road, *"Jordie! COME BACK!"* Still no response. Suddenly, a car appeared from nowhere and struck the animal. He went underneath the vehicle and was thrust out the back. It was as though I watched it happen in slow motion. I couldn't believe what I was seeing. I dropped my new surfboard on the sidewalk and ran out onto the road, picked up my beloved dog, ran home, and sat at the end of our long driveway.

Blood was dripping from his mouth, and there was a hole in the unconscious animal's head. The car that had hit the dog stopped opposite the driveway. A distraught man got out, walked over to me, put one hand on my shoulder, and burst into tears. No one ate Sue's dinner that night.

Phillip, my older brother and I rushed the animal to the local veterinarian, where a day later they put him to sleep (the dog, that is). That night I thought about God. Death tends to make us do that, even if it's just the death of a dog.

Sue and I were married in 1970, and late in 1971, something happened that changed my life forever. After she drifted off to sleep one night, I looked at her and thought, *I am part of the ultimate statistic. Ten out of ten die. I have everything I want in life—my own business, a car, my own house, freedom to do what I want when I want, and a beautiful wife, but death is going to tear from my hands everything I hold dear to me.* I sat on the edge of the bed and wept at the futility of life.

I then decided to do all I could to ensure that I lived a long, healthy life. I visited my local doctor to ask him how I could remain well—and noticed that he looked deathly sick as he sat behind his desk and breathed in the burning fumes of a cigarette. He became a mortal statistic a few years later.

I then looked to science for an answer to my dilemma—and noticed that scientists were more concerned about putting a man on the moon than they were about the fact that death awaited all of us. There seemed to be no answer to the problem of death. I resigned myself to my utter futility and hopelessness.

Six months later (April 1972), Sue kindly allowed me to leave her and our newborn son at home and go on a surfing trip with friends. Five of us traveled about a hundred miles north of my home. One of them was a Christian.

On the second night, I found myself in Graeme Reid's room, talking about the things of God. Earlier that evening I had read the words of Jesus: "You have heard that it was said by them of old, 'You shall not commit adultery'" and had mumbled, "Good. If there's a heaven, I will probably get there, because I haven't committed adultery." But then I read something that cut me in two: "But I say to you, that whoever looks upon a woman to lust after her has committed adultery already with her in his heart." I was shocked. I thought, *Does God see my thought-life? Has He seen what I am really like? If He is going to judge me by that standard—that lust is adultery—I'm not going to make it to heaven. I will end up in hell!*

I remembered one incident that happened some months earlier in my store. A young lady had wanted me to make her a leather miniskirt, and as I measured her hips I became nervous. My fear was of committing adultery. I was happily married, but there was something in me that I couldn't identify, that seemed to consume my want to do good.

After reading Matthew 5:27–28 on a surfing trip with some friends, I was devastated. It was around 9 p.m. on the first night of our trip. We were all pretty exhausted after a day of surfing. I was in one room and Graeme was presumably fast asleep in another. But I *had* to talk with him. I cracked open his door. Wayne was fast asleep. I whispered, "Graeme, are you awake?"

"Yes. Wanna talk?"

He beckoned me in, and we began to talk about life and death. Wayne stirred at the sound of our whispering voices; mumbled, "Huh? You guys talking about God? I'm outta here . . . " and quickly exited the room.

I said, "Tell me what the Bible says about death. I don't understand it."

Graeme switched the light on, and in his gentle manner, asked, "So you believe in God?"

"Of course. I pray every night."

"You do?"

"Yes, I do."

"I never thought that you would be interested in the things of God."

"Oh, I have read parts of the Bible; the whole book of Psalms. I actually enjoyed it. I thought about God when my dog died. It sounds kind of funny, but I did. Death doesn't make any sense. Why would God create us, give us so many good things, and then let us all die? It's crazy."

Graeme smiled and said, "We die because we have sinned against God."

"I know that I have sinned. Even as a little kid, I was a thief. We stole from our neighbor's orchards, and as I grew older, I certainly gave myself to lust. Graeme, there's something in me that wants to do wrong, and I don't know why or what it is."

"That's your sinful nature."

"Good description. My nature is *full* of sin. Right now I'm feeling, well, really guilty."

"That's because you are. It's your conscience that's speaking to you. Everything you have ever done is recorded in your memory banks, and God also has a record."

"So what would happen to me if I died right now? What would God do with me?"

Graeme was gentle but firm in his answer. He asked, "What do you think God *should* do with you?"

"I think that if God sees lust as adultery, I would end up in hell. I know I would."

"You are right. Do you understand the cross?"

"What do you mean?"

"Do you understand what God did on the cross?"

"You mean when Jesus died? No I don't. I mean, I believe that He died on a cross and rose again. I don't have any problem with Him being the Son of God. But, no, I don't know what it's about."

Graeme smiled, and said, "Well, let me tell you. When you sinned, you broke God's Law. But when Jesus suffered on the cross, He paid your fine."

"I think it's starting to make sense. Why didn't I see this before? I knew He died, but I didn't know *why* He died. *It was for me*. It was so that I could be forgiven . . . That makes sense!"

"Let me read this to you," Graeme said. "It's Romans 10:8–11: 'But what does it say? 'The word is near you, in your mouth and in your heart' (that is, the word of faith which we preach): that if you confess with your mouth the Lord Jesus and believe in your heart that God has raised Him from the dead, you will be saved. For with the heart one believes unto righteousness, and with the mouth confession is made unto salvation. For the Scripture says, 'Whoever believes on Him will not be put to shame' [NKJV]. God is here now, in this room. If you will repent and call on Him, you will be saved from hell. Do you want to pray?"

"Yes, but what will I say?"

"Whatever you want." He smiled and said, "Here. I will turn the light off to make it easier for you."

With the moonlight streaming through the window I whispered, "God, please forgive me for everything I have done. I know that I have sinned against You. I am so sorry. I never understood the cross. I do now, and I want to give You my life, and I want to thank You for becoming a human being and dying for me."

The next day, I didn't want to go surfing. I wanted to read the Bible. Something had happened. Something so huge I could hardly wrap my mind around it. I had found that for which I was looking. I tried to analyze it. It was like a baby who cries the moment it's delivered. A nurse asks, "Why are you crying?" The newborn says, "I don't know! Something is missing. *Something is missing!*" The nurse picks the infant up and put it on the mother's breast. As the baby begins to suckle, the nurse asks, "Is this what you were looking for?" The baby stops, smiles, and says, "Yes! *This is it.* This was what I was crying out for, but I didn't know it because I had never experienced it before!"

That's how I felt. I had been crying out for God, but I didn't know what I was looking for because I had never experienced Him before.

There was another way I could explain it. The ultimate in surfing is to get "covered" in the tube by a wave. It's what surfers live for. It's the "rush" in surfing. When that happens, a surfer will often lift his hands in ecstasy. I had that very same feeling from the moment I repented and trusted in Jesus. It was a bubbly joy, it didn't go away, and I didn't have to get cold, wet, and dangle my feet as shark bait to get it.

As I began to read the Bible, it explained what had happened to me. Death had lost its sting. God had commuted my death sentence. I had everlasting life!

Graeme was astounded. He kept saying over and over, "Ray Comfort, a Christian. I don't believe it!" He couldn't believe it because he thought I was self-sufficient, and because I was happy with my life, I wouldn't be interested in God. I *was* extremely happy, but I could see that all that I had achieved in life was temporal. It was "chasing the wind" (see Ecclesiastes 1:14). But on this unspeakably wonderful night, by God's grace I broke into the eternal! I remember thinking, *This is what I have been looking for! Thank*

You, dear Lord! You heard my cry and saved me from death. You didn't leave me in the dark and hopeless shadow of death. I am so grateful. Words can't express my gratitude. What do You want me to do?

I called Sue and said, "Are you lonely?" She said, "Yes, I am," so I responded, "Well, don't worry . . . God is with you." Sue had been raised in a Christian home, and she knew what had happened to me.

I was a new person. Brand-new. I was no longer drowning in the sea of my own lusts. My feet were established on the rock of the fear of the Lord. Now I had a reason to flee from miniskirt temptation— because I now feared God. When temptation came, I could say with Joseph, "How could I do this thing and sin against God!" (See Genesis 39.)

It was radical when I was born the first time. I didn't exist—then suddenly I did. This new birth was just as radical. I couldn't stop thinking about God, when for the previous twenty-two years I hadn't given Him one moment's serious thought. The Bible suddenly came alive. I had a peace that passed understanding, and a joy that was unspeakable.

I immediately became deeply concerned about the salvation of my loved ones. What would become of my precious mom and dad, my brother and my sister? I was horrified at the thought of *anyone* going to hell, let alone my loved ones. I pleaded with them to come to Christ, but to no avail at that time. It would be thirty-three years before my dad would surrender to the Savior.

I began to share my faith with almost everyone I met. I told my surfing buddies, "I have found something that is better than surfing!" Even though they couldn't conceive of such a thing, more than a dozen gave their lives to Christ.

One day, a ninety-one-year-old Presbyterian minister walked into my store and said, "I hear that you have become a Christian. Congratulations." As he shook my hand, he left ten dollars in it (I liked that man from the moment I met him!)

I was amazed at how close we became as friends— me, a long-haired, scruffy surfer and him, a neatly dressed, ninety-one-year-old minister. But our hearts were knit in Christ.

One day, for some reason, Reverend Densem insisted on buying me a hand-turned mimeograph copier. It was a little strange that he was so insistent, but I decided to make use of it and write a tract. It was called "Sin not Skin," and it pinpointed the root cause of racism. Someone saw it and wanted me to run off five thousand more copies. Looking back, I couldn't have dreamed that I would end up with a ministry that would produce and sell well over 100 million tracts. I thank God for dear old Reverend Densem and his strange gift.

Someone purchased the building that housed my store, and the only other place I could find was six miles from home, in the heart of our city. Although New Zealand is a comparatively Godless nation, my hometown of 350,000 people is called Christchurch (named after Jesus), and it had a church in the center square, surrounded by four parks named after Christian martyrs.

One day I took a bus to work and looked at the faces of those surrounding me. I thought, *All these people are going to die. They are just like me—with the same love of life and fear of death. If they die in their sins they will end up in hell.* I then prayed a very dangerous prayer. I whispered, "Dear God, if only there was a way to reach them; if only there was a place I could preach . . ."

Shortly after the bus incident, a colorful character dressed as a wizard, and calling himself "the Wizard," arrived in Christchurch and embarrassed the town council. The law stated that no one was allowed to speak to crowds in the open air, so he set up a chalkboard and, rather than speaking, he gave people the written word.

The news media loved it and followed the story with great interest. After two weeks of pressure, the authorities designated an area in the heart of the city for public speaking and called it "Speaker's Corner."

When that happened, I thought to myself, *What an answer to prayer*... horrors!" When I was in high school, I had to make a speech in front of the class. My mind went blank right in the middle of the talk, and I had to sit down, humiliated beyond words in front of my peers. I had determined that I would never speak in public again. Ever.

I avoided any thought of Speaker's Corner, until I saw a picture in the newspaper that seemed to jump out and slap my face. Under the picture, it explained that an elderly, violin-playing woman was speaking about her faith to groups of people in the local square. I felt ashamed, and determined to go into the square and speak to the crowd. I did preach that day, and ended up speaking there more than three thousand times—almost daily for twelve years.

It was during those early days of open-air speaking that I attended the funeral of the fifth surfing buddy who died from drug abuse. The sight of John's sister lying across his coffin, screaming out his name, left an indelible impression on my mind. I felt frustrated that so many were being cut off in their youth, so I produced an eight-page pamphlet on the dangers of drug abuse, and called it "My Friends Are Dying!"

A charitable trust heard of my endeavor and gave me a thousand dollars to have more printed to get them into schools. Soon after that came the printing of a book with the same name. I stayed up almost all night for three nights to finish the publication and took it to my printer.

I was in a quandary about how to get publicity for it, as I couldn't afford to advertise. One day the subject came up when I was speaking to my friendly rival, the Wizard (whose photo appeared in the book). He spoke once a week on a popular radio program, "cursing" different things around the country. I quietly suggested, "Why don't you curse my book?" He smiled, said with his raspy voice, "Now, that's a good idea," and took a copy with him.

The following Tuesday I turned on the radio at 8 a.m. and heard, "Ray Comfort's book is crudely written. It has photos of me in it, without my long hair and beard. The publication is pathetic. It's called *My Friends Are Dying!* and you will find it for sale at . . . ," and he named the bookstore. (This book is now titled *Out of the Comfort Zone*).

They completely sold out that morning!

From then on the book received national media attention and opened up an itinerant ministry for me. I began getting hundreds of invitations to speak at schools, churches, and service groups. After speaking on drug prevention, I gave a basic gospel message.

Shortly after its publication I opened the Drug Prevention Center, which was located on High Street—an unfortunate choice of street names for a drug center. This was different from the rehabilitation center. Our aim this time was to *prevent* drug abuse through education, rather than trying to clean up the mess at the other end.

Then churches began to invite me to teach them how to share their faith. I became too busy to make jackets—instead of making five a week, I could only manage one. Fortunately, a local church asked me to become an assistant pastor, so I closed my store and began serving in a local church and traveling most weekends, while still preaching each weekday in the heart of the city.

In 1978, I decided to make a documentary called "My Friends Are Dying." During the filming in the square, two gangs began to fight over a woman. They used knives and an axe, and amazingly my cameraman captured the violent encounter. The film was seized by police, who used it as court evidence.

It was because of my film that many of the gang members were put into prison. It was also because of that sequence that more than two thousand people showed up for the film's premiere. Sometime later, I screened it to the gangs in prison, and preached to them afterwards. They were a captive audience.

Despite the excitement of these incidents, I was very frustrated. Almost all of my surfing buddies who had made commitments to Christ had fallen away from the faith. Many of them had become bitter "backsliders," and I couldn't understand why. As I traveled to different churches and looked at their growth records, I discovered that 90 percent of those making decisions for Christ, in local churches and in large crusades, were falling away from the faith.

One day, I read a portion of a sermon by Charles Spurgeon. This is what he said:

> There is a war between you and God's Law. The Ten Commandments are against you. The first comes forward and says, "Let him be cursed. For he denies Me. He has another god beside Me. His god is his belly and he yields his homage to his lust." All the Ten Commandments, like ten great cannons, are pointed at you today. For you have broken all of God's statutes and lived in daily neglect of all His commands. Soul, thou wilt find it a hard thing to go at war with the Law. When the Law came in peace, Sinai was altogether on

> a smoke and even Moses said, "I exceeding fear and quake!" What will you do when the Law of God comes in terror; when the trumpet of the archangel shall tear you from your grave; when the eyes of God shall burn their way into your guilty soul; when the great books shall be opened and all your sin and shame shall be punished . . . Can you stand against an angry Law in that Day?

I remember thinking, *Wow . . . that's a little different from "God loves you and has a wonderful plan for your life."* I put the thought into my memory banks, and a few days later I was reading Galatians 3:24. However, instead of reading it, "The law was our schoolmaster to bring us to Christ" (KJ2000), I subconsciously read it as "The law was a schoolmaster to bring *Israel* to Christ." The question suddenly struck me: *Is it legitimate to use the Law—the Ten Commandments (as Spurgeon did) as a schoolmaster to bring sinners to Christ—just as it brought Israel to Christ?* It was such a revelation; it almost took my breath away. I closed my Bible and began to search for a sinner on whom I could experiment.

When I found a gentleman who was open to the gospel, I took him through the Ten Commandments first, and *then* I shared the cross. I diagnosed the disease before I gave the cure. He stood to his feet and said, "I've never heard anyone put that so clearly in all my life." It was like a light went on in both of our heads. He understood the gospel, and I began to understand the great principle that the Law is a schoolmaster that brings the knowledge of sin, convincing a sinner of his need for the Savior.

I immediately began to search the literature of men like John Wesley, Spurgeon, Whitefield, Luther, and others whom God had used down through the ages, and found that each warned that if the Law wasn't used to prepare the way for the gospel, sinners would fall away, and the Church would also fill with false converts.

I began to pull together a one-hour sermon called "Hell's Best-Kept Secret" that began with the statistics I had uncovered, then told the story of a youth who broke a speeding law and had no money to pay his fine. It explained the place of civil law, and then God's Law, relating it to Jesus paying our fine so that we could leave God's courtroom.

In 1986, Sue and I flew to Hawaii, and I had the privilege of sharing the teaching with a group of missionaries. The organization so appreciated what they heard that over the next few years, they flew us back eight times.

It was during one of those trips that a pastor from California sat in the session, disagreed with what I said at first, but after studying the Scriptures, he called me in New Zealand and said, "America must hear this message! Please pray about bringing this teaching to this country." I knew it was in God's timing.

In January 1989, I uprooted my family from our home country and flew seven thousand miles to the United States with the sole purpose of bringing "Hell's Best-Kept Secret" to America.

Things were relatively quiet for the first three years. I spent much of my time feeding the homeless and bathing the wounds of drug addicts at the famous MacArthur Park. Little did I know when I went there that it was known for having the highest murder rate in Los Angeles. It began to dawn on me that it wasn't the safest of places when a drug addict advised me to preach with my back to a tree so I wouldn't get stabbed. Looking back, I can see that I was very naive. I kept a daily diary of what happened and republished *My Friends Are Dying* under the title *Out of the Comfort Zone*. That helped fill in my time as I waited for God to open doors for "Hell's Best-Kept Secret."

In 1992, I received a call from Bill Gothard in Chicago. I had heard of him when I was in New Zealand but wasn't familiar with his voice. Friends knew that I felt frustrated as I waited for God to open doors, and they called—pretending to be Billy Graham and asking if I wanted to speak at a crusade. So when a voice I had never heard said that he was Bill Gothard, I thought it was one of my friends kidding me, and for about sixty seconds I was waiting for a gap so I could say, "Yeah, and I'm Elvis. I'll see you at Disneyland." Fortunately, I didn't find a gap. Someone had given him a tape of "Hell's Best-Kept Secret," and he thought the teaching was so important that the following week he flew me to San Jose, California, and had me share it with a thousand pastors. He put the teaching on video, and in 1993 he screened it to thirty thousand pastors. From then on doors began to open.

Also in 1992, David Wilkerson called. He had been listening to "Hell's Best-Kept Secret" in his car, and called me on his car phone. This was a famous voice I was very familiar with. He immediately flew me three thousand miles, from Los Angeles to New York, to share the one-hour teaching with his church. He considered it to be *that* important.

When I preached in New Zealand, I wore a T-shirt that said "I don't believe in atheists," so I decided to develop the thought and write a book called *God Doesn't Believe in Atheists*. When I sent the manuscript to a publisher, the owner gave it to his atheist son-in-law to read, and God saved him as he read it—so they immediately published the book.

It was because I had written tracts and the book that I decided to write to American Atheists, Inc., and ask them if they would allow me to speak at one of their conventions. Not surprisingly, they turned me down, but their national spokesperson began to e-mail me. At one point he asked, "Would you have the courage to face me in a debate, at our national convention?" I told him that I would be honored and would even pay my own airfare from Los Angeles to Florida. Then I sent him a copy of *God Doesn't Believe in Atheists* so he would have some material to argue against me.

A week later he withdrew from the debate. Then an atheist wrote and accused me of being the one who backed down. I said, "Hey, it wasn't me who chickened out. It was Ron Barrier—your national spokesperson." I then sent him Ron's original e-mail, and Mr. Barrier became *roast* chicken. He reinstated the offer, flew me from Los Angeles to Florida, and put me in a nice hotel. They even had a fruit basket waiting for me (I took along a food-taster to be safe).

The debate was on Good Friday of 2001. It went very well. The group let me present the gospel to two hundred of their members, and broadcast it *live* over the Internet. We hugged afterwards, and I even had the strange experience of signing my book for atheists.

In October 2001, I received a phone call that would change my life and ministry. It was from well-known Hollywood actor Kirk Cameron. Someone had given Kirk "Hell's Best-Kept Secret" and, after listening to it twice, he suddenly understood the importance of its message, called me, and we spent three hours over lunch.

I then sent him some further reading material. It was a book I had written called *God Has a Wonderful Plan for Your Life: The Myth of the Modern Message*, and had a cover graphic of Stephen being stoned to death. It was the fact that Kirk couldn't reconcile the picture with the title that provoked him to read the book. That night God used the book to transform his life. The next day he e-mailed me and said:

> Ray, I was so fired up after leaving your place! Your teachings on the Law and grace have made more sense to me than anyone else's, and I am so thankful for what God is doing . . . I believe I was robbed of the deep pain of seeing the depth of my sinfulness, of experiencing the exceeding joy and gratitude that comes from the cross, because I was convinced of God's love before I was convinced of my sin. I didn't see the big problem, but by faith believed I was a sinner (many worse than me, but nevertheless a sinner), and repented of my "general sinful, selfish attitude." I had never

opened up the Ten Commandments and looked deep into the well of my sinful heart. I never imagined that God was actually angry with me at a certain point because of my sin. Because of "grace," I kind of skipped over that part and was just thankful that He loved me and had promised me eternal life. While I think I was saved thirteen years ago, I was rocked out of my chair last night, on my knees confessing the specific sins that have plagued my heart that were never uncovered before. I think my knowledge of the "new covenant" and "under grace, not Law" kept me from ever examining my heart by the light of the Ten Commandments. The new weight of my sin is causing more pain in me . . . wounding my ego, and showing me how much more Jesus had to pay to set me free. Oh, the wonderful cross!

From then on, we combined ministries, and for the next year Kirk must have said a dozen times, "How can we get this teaching to the Church?" I answered him the same way almost every time—"Welcome to Club Frustration." Despite the opening of many doors, we felt as though we had made limited progress.

It seems that God heeded our combined frustration. In 2002, through a series of amazing circumstances, Kirk taught "Hell's Best-Kept Secret" *live* (from my teaching notes) on the world's largest Christian television network.

Our website received more than a million hits, in

just one day! The network couldn't believe how their ratings went through the roof. Many channel surfers had beached themselves on the Christian network when they saw their favorite sitcom star at a pulpit. The network pleaded with him to host a regular program, but he suggested that we instead produce our own TV program, teaching Christians how to share their faith biblically. So that's what we did. We produced a television program called *The Way of the Master*, which is, as of this writing, in its fourth season, is on thirty networks, is aired in seventy countries, and, to our delight, has won seven awards.

Meanwhile, my relationship with atheists blossomed. One of our booklets is called *The Atheist Test* and has sold more than a million copies. Some courageous Christian dropped forty of them at a dinner where forty atheists had gathered for fellowship and food. After reading the booklet, they contacted me and invited me to join them for dinner.

I took a friend and determined not to argue with these people, but to love them. During the meal, I had the bill delivered to me and quietly paid it. I was so thrilled as I did so, my hands almost shook with excitement. The leaders were stunned that I had covered the cost for the whole dinner, and I had the joy of having atheists come to me and whisper as they left, "Thank you, Mr. Comfort, for paying for dinner." As we left that place that night, we clicked our heels with joy. A quiet display of Christian love can sometimes be more powerful than the most eloquent of sermons or the most powerful of arguments.

In 2007, I started a blog called *Atheist Central*. Every day, hundreds of atheists read what I have written and rip it to pieces. Each Sunday, we even have "Atheist Church" on the blog, along with a hymn (via YouTube), and sermons directed at atheists, special announcements, and, of course, a benediction.

I have even gone back to making leather jackets and vests, and I am freely giving them to atheists who want them. Each week we have a draw, and the lucky atheist gets free handmade leather wear, and I must say that I get far more joy making jackets for atheists than I ever did when I was making them for money. My hope is that they will see that I genuinely care about them—that I am in earnest when I warn them about the reality of hell and speak of the incredible offer of heaven.

Do you remember my old friend—the Reverend George Densem? A few years after we met, while I was still living in Christchurch, his wife called, said that he was on his deathbed, and asked if I could possibly be with him at this time. I told her that I would be honored.

A few minutes later, she ushered me into his bedroom. His wife was on the phone, which was right by the bedroom door. It had a loud ring, because George was partly deaf. As he lay in bed without his teeth, he looked pretty bad. I sat beside him and whispered, "It's me, George . . . Ray. I have come to be with you."

George said, "I'm going to be with Jesus, Ray." I sat there quietly, holding his hand and thinking, *What an honor I have . . . to be present when a saint goes marching through to glory. I wonder how he will go, Lord. I wonder how he will go . . .*

After twenty minutes, George raised his right hand, pointed to the heavens, and said, "Jesus said, 'I am the way, the truth and the life . . .'" Then he sighed deeply as though it were his last breath. I whispered, "Wow! *What a way to go!*"

Suddenly, the phone rang, George sat up, and I was the one who just about died! *He lasted for another two years!*

But when he did go, I went to his funeral, and they sang, "To God be the glory, great things He has done. So loved He the world that He gave us His Son, who yielded His life, an atonement for sin, and opened the life gate that all may go in."

What an incredible gospel we have! Death has lost its sting! Like the disciples, we cannot but speak of that which we have seen and heard. God has offered everlasting life to dying humanity! How can we remain silent?

・ 17 ・

THE FEAR OF DYING:

EINSTEIN'S LAST

WORDS

I do not believe in immortality of the individual, and I consider ethics to be an exclusively human concern with no superhuman authority behind it.[1]

—Albert Einstein

*A*N ATHEIST ONCE WROTE and asked, "Ray, are you afraid of dying?" This is perhaps the shortest question I've been asked, but I will probably give it one of my longest answers, because it's a question with which every sane person wrestles. So I will be thoughtful and very candid with my answer.

The quick response is, "Yes, I am fearful, and no, I'm not." I am not afraid of dying, but I am afraid of the *process* of dying (as I have noted that a number of atheists have also said).

Back on December 5, 2009, I turned sixty. That was six decades and nine months of life. When I turned twenty, I was shocked. It took me by surprise. I loved being a carefree teenager, and it was suddenly gone.

When I turned forty, I was quietly horrified. People who were forty were "middle-aged." They were balding, potbellied, and it seemed to me that they were past the exciting adventure of life.

But when I turned sixty, I was quietly philosophical. I'd had time to give this one much deep thought.

There are some good things about getting old. Sue and I can enjoy those good old black-and-white movies again and again, for the first time.

There is also a blessing of being around to turn sixty. I have friends who didn't even make it to fifty. One was killed in a bus accident. It rolled on him. Another drowned in shallow water when he hit his head on a rock. Another was killed in a plane accident. Others went with cancer or drugs. Most of us know someone cancer took in his or her youth, or someone who tragically died in a car accident.

When the Beatles sang "When I'm Sixty-Four," I'm sure they never thought that two of them wouldn't get to sixty-four. The "when" never came. One went quickly with a bullet; the other, slowly with cancer. Every year forty thousand unfortunate Americans are killed on the roads, and statistics tell us that around eighteen thousand are murdered, and hundreds of thousands die of cancer and other terrible diseases.

Then there are those who die in warfare. Millions have been cut off in their twenties with a bullet or a bomb, and the majority of those didn't even experience the joy of having kids, let alone growing old.

I was very aware that when I turned sixty, I would be entering the decade of loss. I would begin to lose any youthful looks that I had left. Any muscle strength I had before would quickly diminish. My skin would become loose and lifeless. My eyesight would begin to go. So would my hearing, thought process, memory, and taste buds. My immune system would weaken and make me vulnerable to a stack of terrible terminal diseases.

These depressing things happen to everyone, despite regular exercise, daily juicing, and consuming a careful diet. No one can beat this rap. All this and much more will come in the next twenty years, if death doesn't come to me first through a heart attack or aneurism or 101 other unexpected surprises.

So "the process of dying" isn't a matter of a few weeks on a hospital deathbed. It happens over twenty or so years.

In one of Spielberg's memorable movies (if my memory is to be trusted), the aging process happened to one evil character in an instant of time. He had to choose the cup from which Jesus drank at the Last Supper (the Holy Grail). He believed that if he drank from it, he would live forever. He quickly grabbed the most attractive golden cup and began to drink. He wasn't perceptive enough to realize that Jesus was a lowly carpenter and would have had a simple, humble wooden cup. The moment he took it to his lips, he aged from a healthy forty-year-old to a dry and dusty skeleton that crumpled to the ground.

The immediate outlook in life for *any* of us (even for the most optimistic of positive thinkers and health-conscious juice drinkers—whether Christian or atheist) is pretty gloomy.

So, am I afraid of this process of dying? Part of the answer is that I'm about as afraid as a faithful soldier, as he goes into a battle from which he is certain he will not return. His is a natural and understandable human emotion, because he loves life and deeply values those he loves. Only a shallow-thinking person would have no fear.

But here now is the most important and exciting part of my answer.

Almost every skeptic makes a huge mistake when it comes to the issue of faith. He thinks that a Christian is someone who believes in the existence of God despite an overwhelming lack of evidence. That's why he chooses to be an unbeliever. He never seems to be able to differentiate between *intellectual faith* and *implicit trust.*

Let's say I step into an elevator on the eighty-fourth floor of a massive high-rise. I have just entrusted my life to it. Any apprehension I have will be in proportion to the trust I exercise. If I have no trust in the elevator, I will have a ton of fear. If I have absolute trust, I will have no fear at all.

The ingredient that makes the difference between the two states of mind is knowledge. If I know that the elevator is state-of-the-art, is computer operated, and is checked daily, and I *believe* what I know, my trust will grow.

But if I *personally* inspect the twelve three-inch-thick, unbreakable steel cables that hold each elevator, my trust will grow more. If I understand that the computer system has a backup, and immediately shuts down the elevator and calls inspectors at the first hint of trouble, my trust will grow even greater. The more trust I have, the less fear will have room to plague me.

However, if I *choose* not to believe what I am shown about the computer system, the cables, the inspections, and so forth, I will be plagued by my fears. My trust in the elevator is a choice, based on knowledge that is simply believed. Remember, the knowledge I have is more than a belief that the elevator exists.

So when it comes to the issue of God and salvation, the die-hard skeptic disqualifies himself before he even begins. By choice, he refuses to intellectually believe that God exists, despite the overwhelming and axiomatic evidence of creation and the moral nature of the God-given conscience.

So if you truly believe that God doesn't exist (which I doubt), you may as well stop reading at this point, because you are in the category of what the Bible calls "unreasonable" (see 2 Thessalonians 3:2). But for the *reasonable* skeptic who understands that his or her existence is indeed hopeless (in the truest sense of the word), there is a wonderful hope. So please stay with me. Just keep in mind that it is essential that you understand that the trust a Christian has in God is *not* the belief that He exists.

Here's how the trusting Christian deals with the fear of death. He possesses the knowledge that God *cannot* lie. He knows that He is morally perfect. That means He is without sin. As the Scriptures say, "In Him is no darkness at all" (1 John 1:5 NKJV). The eighteen-mile-thick, unbreakable titanium cables of His promises are absolutely worthy of the Christian's trust. There is no doubt of that. The believer *knows* the reality of the verse "He is faithful that promised" (Hebrews 10:23 KJV). When fear comes, it cannot get past this knowledge, and that results in trust. Such trust comes as a gift at the point of conversion. It is part of the new birth of John 3.

The more the Christian trusts the promises of God, the less fear he has. The two are incompatible. That means that the trusting Christian can say with the apostle Paul, "I *know* and *believe* and am *persuaded* that He is able to keep that which I am committed unto him (my life) against the Day (Judgment Day)" (see 2 Timothy 1:12). He is saved from death and the just deserts of his sin.

That leaves the faithless skeptic alone with his fears. He has refused knowledge of the faithfulness of God, so he is left with certain tormenting uncertainties. Often, his pride will never permit him to admit that he has any fears, but they will come. He doesn't realize that fear *has torment* as the Bible says (see 1 John 4:18). He has forgotten what it is like to wake up after a terrifying nightmare. Sometimes it takes about ten minutes after waking up just to shake off such gripping fears. And when it comes to the subject of trust in God, the unbeliever has no power to stop fear from gripping his very soul to the core, because he refused the antidote of faith.

The seed of fear torments with a question. It whispers, "What if?" *What if* Jesus spoke the truth and God *does* consider lust to be adultery? What if He *does* see hatred as murder? What if He *has* seen and remembered every single secret sin, and every sinful imagination of the heart? What if hell *does* exist? *What if* that silly little, anti-science, money-hungry, lying, stealing, fanatical, banana-man idiot-preacher was actually speaking the truth?

Millions know what it is to be paralyzed by a tormenting fear. It drives them to insanity, to drink, and it even drives many to suicide to escape its torment. If you are so unwise as to leave yourself without faith in Jesus, you will not be able to stand against it. The Bible calls death "the king of terrors," and I have seen it terrorize grown men who have rejected God. It is fearful to see, but much, much worse to experience.

So, whatever you do in this precious life of yours, don't reject the Savior and die in your sins. God has made the way to be saved very simple. He says that each of us is in terrible danger, and He kindly provided a way for us to get what we don't deserve. That's called "mercy." We can avoid the just desert of hell, and instead have the undeserved gift of everlasting life. But whatever you do, don't get "religious." Don't try to clean up your life. You and I are like the thief on the cross. He couldn't go anywhere; he couldn't do anything. He was pinned to the cross by the unforgiving nails of Roman civil law. All he could do was turn to Jesus and say, "Lord, remember me . . ."

In the same way, we can't do anything to save ourselves, because we are condemned by the merciless Law of God. All we can do is turn to Jesus and say, "Lord, remember me . . ." The moment you come to know Him as Lord and trust Him as Savior, you will forever banish any what-ifs. Again, this is because faith comes as a gift from God. He will *give* you faith. He will help you in your unbelief by giving you a new heart and new desires. You will *want* to love, trust in, and obey everything God would have you to do. And a total trust doesn't allow any fear, in the light of the knowledge of God. Fear is for unbelievers.

Always keep in mind that the most important

moment of your life will be the instant of your death. Don't be like the man who neglected his eternal salvation. Jesus said that God said, "You fool. Tonight your soul shall be required of you" (Luke 12:20, paraphrased). In other words there's a debt that has to be paid. Hell required him. Death wanted its wages.

If you are considering these thoughts, please don't worry about what your unbelieving friends or family think. Worry about what *God* thinks. If they are your friends, they will respect you no matter what you believe. But if they turn on you like a pack of vicious hyenas, they were never your friends in the first place. You will have lost nothing.

Your life is without price, and you will lose it without the Savior. Seek Him with all of your heart. Jesus suffered and died on a cruel cross so that God could extend mercy toward you. He rose from the dead so you could live free from the fear of and the power of death. His gift to you is eternal life. Such is God's love for you. Do you believe that? For your sake I hope you do.

So make sure you choose the Carpenter's cup. Choose to trust Jesus Christ. Confess and forsake your sins and willfully put your reliance (your trust) in Jesus right now, and you will come to know Him in whom life is eternal. I can't express to you what a joy it is to me, what amazing consolation, what an absolute hope I have in Christ. Death has lost its sting completely. This is how Scripture explains it:

> For which cause we faint not; but though our outward man perish, yet the inward man is renewed day by day. For our light affliction, which is but for a moment, works for us a far more exceeding and eternal weight of glory; while we look not at the things which are seen, but at the things which are not seen: for the things which are seen are temporal; but the things which are not seen are eternal. (2 Corinthians 4:16–18 KJV)

You had no choice in being born. You just found yourself alive. You had no choice where you were to be born. You just found yourself in a certain country, speaking a certain language. You didn't choose your looks or your personality. But this day, God Himself gives you a choice in your eternal destiny. Choose wisely. (See www.needGod.com for further information.)

***

Albert Einstein died on April 18, 1955, after experiencing internal bleeding that was caused by the rupture of an abdominal aortic aneurysm. He refused the offer of surgery, saying, "I want to go when I want. It is tasteless to prolong life artificially. I have done my share, it is time to go. I will do it elegantly."[2]

He once said, "It's not that I'm so smart, it's just that I stay with problems longer." Death was a problem he couldn't solve. Einstein tragically died in Princeton Hospital in the early hours of the morning, at the age of seventy-six.

Will we see him in heaven? Perhaps. He had tremendous respect for the Savior. He had once said, when asked, "You accept the historical existence of Jesus?" "Unquestionably! No one can read the Gospels without feeling the actual presence of Jesus. His personality pulsates in every word. No myth is filled with such life."[3] In the same interview, the host said, "Ludwig Lewisohn, in one of his recent books, claims that many of the sayings of Jesus paraphrase the sayings of other prophets."

"No man," Einstein replied, "can deny the fact that Jesus existed, nor that his sayings are beautiful. Even if some them have been said before, no one has expressed them so divinely as he."[4]

More important, he didn't die instantly in a head-on collision. He had time to consider his mortality. As he neared death, when the adulations of the world had died down and he left his trophies behind, perhaps he reflected on his youthful boasting: "I have firmly resolved to bite the dust, when my time comes, with the minimum of medical assistance, and up to then I will sin to my wicked heart's content."[5] Perhaps he remembered the many times he'd committed adultery, and abandoned his wife and children for another woman. Maybe he personalized his words: "The real problem is in the hearts and minds of men. It is easier to denature plutonium than to denature the evil spirit of man." It may have been that he thought about his advice to others—"Never do anything against conscience even if the state demands it"[6] or "True religion is real living; living with all one's soul, with all one's goodness and righteousness."

Perhaps as the great genius lay on his deathbed, his mind went back to August 1914, when he wrote to a friend who had lost his mother:

Dear friend Zangger,

My deepest condolences on the heavy loss you suffered. I knew your dear mother as an excellent mother. I saw many a tear in her eye when you were so sick and an indescribable joy on her face when you were slowly regaining your strength. It never became clear to me where your refinement and sensitivity and your quick reflexes came from, besides the Germanic blood coursing through your veins. What a horrific picture the world is now offering! Nowhere is there an island of culture where people have retained human feeling. Nothing but hate and a lust for power! The question, where can justice

be found? is becoming sheer mockery. One lives
the life of a stranger on this planet, happy when
one isn't done in for outmoded sentiments. I feel
so strangely drawn to early Christianity and feel
as acutely as never before how much nicer it is
to be anvil than hammer. What galls me most is
that now even the best talent is being forced into
this senseless butchery and henchman's service.
I have blind luck to thank that I was spared this.[7]

Einstein then felt "drawn to early Christianity."
Death tends to remind us of God. It was the death
of my dog that made me first seriously think of Him.
Nothing and no one else can help us with the impasse
of death. Perhaps such thoughts brought him back to
early Christianity—to the foot of a bloodstained cross.
For the man who was known for his profound thoughts,
maybe he wasn't thinking too deeply when *Time*
magazine asked him "Do you believe in immortality?"
and he answered, "No. And one life is enough for me."[8]

When Einstein died on that April day, he left a
piece of writing ending in an unfinished sentence.
He had taken the draft of a speech he was preparing
for a television appearance commemorating the
State of Israel's seventh anniversary, but he didn't
live long enough to complete it. These were his last
written words:

In essence, the conflict that exists today is no more than an old-style struggle for power, once again presented to mankind in semi religious trappings. The difference is that, this time, the development of atomic power has imbued the struggle with a ghostly character; for both parties know and admit that, should the quarrel deteriorate into actual war, mankind is doomed. Despite this knowledge, statesmen in responsible positions on both sides continue to employ the well-known technique of seeking to intimidate and demoralize the opponent by marshaling superior military strength. They do so even though such a policy entails the risk of war and doom. Not one statesman in a position of responsibility has dared to pursue the only course that holds out any promise of peace, the course of supranational security, since for a statesman to follow such a course would be tantamount to political suicide. Political passions, once they have been fanned into flame, exact their victims ... Citater fra ...

Some hours later, as Albert Einstein lay dying in Princeton Hospital, he uttered his last words. Unfortunately, they were in German, and the nurse assigned to him spoke no German. The final words of the greatest physicist of all time were therefore never understood nor recorded.

For a catalog of Ray Comfort's resources, conferences, and training Academy, visit www.livingwaters.com, call 800-437-1893, or write to: Living Waters Publications, P.O. Box 1172, Bellflower, CA 90707, USA. Be sure to sign up for the weekly update online.

Notes

FOREWORD

1. "Barna Survey Examines Changes in Worldview Among Christians over the Past 13 Years," March 9, 2009, Barna Group, accessed January 9, 2014, https://www.barna.org/barna-update/article/21-transformation/252-barna-survey-examines-changes-in-worldview-among-christians-over-the-past-13-years#.UoEtEDQo7IU

2. Richard Dawkins, The God Delusion (New York: Houghton Mifflin, 2006), p. 176. To be fair, Dawkins sometimes likes to describe his belief system as "non-theist."

3. Richard Dawkins speaking on atheism on the Al Jazeera TV network, December 21, 2012, http://www.youtube.com/watch?v=c1iSxEtgEGs.

4. Jörg Blech, "The New Atheists: Researchers Crusade against American Fundamentalists," Speigel Online International, accessed January 9, 2014, http://www.spiegel.de/international/spiegel/the-new-atheists-researchers-crusade-against-american-fundamentalists-a-444787.html.

5. "Richard Dawkins launches children's summer camp for atheists," *Daily Mail, June 28, 2009, accessed January 9, 2014, http://www.dailymail.co.uk/news/article-1196063/Richard-Dawkins-launches-childrens-summer-camp-atheists.html.*

INTRODUCTION

1.   Lacey Rose and Dorothy Pomerantz, "Top-Earning Dead
     Celebrities," *Forbes*, October 27, 2009, http://www.forbes.
     com/2009/10/27/top-earning-dead-celebrities-list-dead-celebs-
     09-business-entertainment-intro.html.
2.   These tracts are available through wwwlivingwaters.com.
3.   See www.livingwaters.com/learn/.

EPIGRAPH

1.   E. Salaman, "A Talk with Einstein," *The Listener* 54 (1955):
     370–71.

CHAPTER 1: EINSTEIN'S HISTORY: THE
EARLY YEARS

1.   Gilbert Fowler White, *Journal of France and Germany* (1942–
     1944), quoted in Robert E. Hinshaw, *Living with Nature's
     Extremes: The Life of Gilbert Fowler White* (n.p.: Johnson
     Books, 2006), 62.
2.   Albert Einstein Anecdotes, http://oaks.nvg.org/sa5ra17.html.
3.   John Stachtel et al., *The Collected Papers of Albert Einstein*,
     vol. 1: *The Early Years, 1879–1902* (Princeton University Press,
     1987), doc. 79.
4.   "Short Life History: Lieserl Einstein-Maric," Albert Einstein
     in the World Wide Web, http://www.einstein-website.de/biog-
     raphies/einsteinlieserl.html, accessed October 22, 2013.
5.   Walter Sullivan, "Einstein Letters Tell of Anguished Love
     Affair," *New York Times*, May 3, 1987, http://www.nytimes.
     com/1987/05/03/us/einstein-letters-tell-of-anguished-love-
     affair.html?pagewanted=3, p. 3.
6.   Ibid., 2.
7.   Abraham Pais, *Subtle Is the Lord . . . The Science and the Life
     of Albert Einstein* (London: Oxford University Press, 1982), 179.

8. William Wallace Campbell (April 11, 1862–June 14, 1938) was an American astronomer, and director of Lick Observatory from 1900 to 1930. A specialist in spectroscopy, Campbell was a pioneer of astronomical spectroscopy and catalogued the radial velocities of stars.

CHAPTER 2: EINSTEIN'S YEARS OF HOPE

1. Walter Isaacson, *Einstein: His Life and Universe*, 1st paperback ed. (New York: Simon & Schuster, 2008), 185.
2. Ibid., 186.
3. Ibid.
4. Walter Isaacson, "The Intimate Life of A. Einstein," *Time* magazine, July 9, 2006, http://www.time.com/time/magazine/article/0,9171,1211594,00.html, p. 1.
5. Ibid., 2.
6. Diana Kormos Buchwald, et al., eds., *The Collected Papers of Albert Einstein*, vol. 10: *The Berlin Years* (Princeton University, 2006), English translation of selected texts, http://press.princeton.edu/chapters/s8332.pdf, 18–19.
7. Isaacson, "The Intimate Life of A. Einstein," 6.
8. Ibid.
9. The Prussian Academy of Sciences was established in Berlin on July 11, 1700.
10. David Hilbert (January 23, 1862–February 14, 1943) was a German mathematician, recognized as one of the most influential and universal mathematicians of the nineteenth and early twentieth centuries. He discovered and developed a broad range of fundamental ideas in many areas, including invariant theory and the axiomatization of geometry.
11. Isaacson, "The Intimate Life of Albert Einstein," 1.
12. Sir Arthur Stanley Eddington (December 28, 1882–November 22, 1944) was an early-twentieth-century British astrophysicist. The Eddington limit, the natural limit to the luminosity of stars, or the radiation generated by accretion onto a compact object, is named in his honor. He is famous for his work regarding the theory of relativity. Eddington wrote a number of articles that announced and explained Einstein's theory of general relativity to the English-speaking world.

13. Jeffrey Crelinsten, *Einstein's Jury: The Race to Test Relativity* (Princeton: Princeton University Press, 2006), 141.

14. "The Nobel Prize in Physics 1921: Albert Einstein," official website of the Nobel Prize, http://www.nobelprize.org/nobel_prizes/physics/laureates/1921/; accessed October 22, 2013.

15. Karen C. Fox and Aries Keck, *Einstein A to Z* (Hoboken, NJ: John Wiley & Sons, 2004), 51. After this incident, Hans Albert had then immigrated to the United States, where he became a professor of hydraulic engineering at UC Berkeley, in California. Years later, even when both father and son were living in America, they remained estranged. When Einstein died in 1955, he left very little wealth to his son.

CHAPTER 3: EINSTEIN'S BELIEF IN GOD

1. Albert Einstein, obituary in *New York Times*, April 19, 1955, quoted in James A. Haught, "Breaking the Last Taboo," *Free Inquiry*, Winter 1996–97.

2. E. Salaman, "A Talk with Einstein," *The Listener* 54 (1955): 370–71.

3. Quoted in Leopold Infeld, *Quest: An Autobiography*, 2nd ed. (Providence: AMS Chelsea, 2006), 279.

4. Quoted in Peter A. Bucky and Allen G. Weakland, *The Private Albert Einstein* (n.p.: Andrews McMeel, 1993), 86.

5. Einstein, in an interview with William Hermanns in the summer of 1954, quoted in *Famous Quotes from 100 Great People* (MobileReference, 2011).

6. Einstein, letter in response to sixth-grader Phyllis Wright's question regarding whether scientists pray, and if so, what they pray for, January 24, 1936, in Walter Isaacson, *Einstein: His Life and Universe* (New York: Simon & Schuster, 2007), 388.

7. Einstein, quoted in William Hermanns, *Einstein and the Poet: In Search of the Cosmic Man* (Wellesley, MA: Branden Books, 1983, 2013), 64.

8. Einstein, remark made during Einstein's first visit to Princeton University, April 1921, quoted in Ronald W. Clark, *Einstein: The Life and Times* (n.p.: Hodder & Stoughton, 1973). *Wikiquote* shows that variant translations of this include: "God is slick, but he ain't mean" and "God is subtle but he is not malicious" (unsourced), http://en.wikiquote.org/wiki/Albert_Einstein, accessed October 22, 2013.

9.   Jessica Ravitz, "Einstein Letter, Set for Auction, Shows Scientist Challenging Idea of God, Being 'Chosen,'" *belief* (CNN blog), October 4, 2012, http://religion.blogs.cnn.com/2012/10/04/einstein-letter-set-for-auction-shows-scientist-challenging-idea-of-god-being-chosen/?hpt=hp_c2.

10. Einstein, letter to Guy H. Raner Jr., September 28, 1949, quoted by Michael R. Gilmore in "Just What Did Einstein Believe about God?" *Skeptic* 5, no. 2 (1997).

11. Prince Hubertus zu Löwenstein, *Towards the Further Shore* (London: Victor Gollancz, 1968), 156, in Max Jammer, *Einstein and Religion: Physics and Theology* (Princeton: Princeton Univ. Press, 2007), 97.

12. Richard Dawkins, *The God Delusion* (London: Transworld, 2006), 34.

13. Einstein, in response to a question about whether or not he believed in God, quoted in George Sylvester Viereck, *Glimpses of the Great* (n.p.: Macaulay, 1930).

14. Einstein to an unidentified addressee, August 7, 1941, Einstein Archive, reel 54-927, in Jammer, *Einstein and Religion*, 97.

15. Richard Dawkins, "Albert Einstein's Historic 1954 'God Letter'," posted on the website of Richard Dawkins Foundation for Reason and Science, September 17, 2012, http://richarddawkins.net/news_articles/2012/8/15/albert-einstein-s-historic-1954-god-letter-handwritten-shortly-before-his-death.

16. http://aa.usno.navy.mil/cgi-bin/aa_rstablew.pl. No longer accessible.

17. http://www.ffrf.org/fttoday/2004/nov/raner.php. No longer accessible. This quotation appears in multiple places on the web.

18. Einstein, letter to Guy H. Raner Jr., July 2, 1945, in Gilmore, "Just What Did Einstein Believe about God?"

19. http://www.ffrf.org/fttoday/2004/nov/raner.php. No longer accessible, but the quote can be found at multiple other sites.

20. Einstein, *Words of Albert Einstein*, trans. Megh Nad Saha (MobileReference, 2010).

21. From Alice Calaprice, *The Expanded Quotable Einstein* (Princeton: Princeton University, 2000), 214; emphasis added.

22. Richard Dawkins, *The God Delusion*, 1st Mariner Books ed. (New York: Houghton Mifflin, 2006; repr., Mariner Books, 2008), 34; emphasis added.

23. Einstein in Viereck, *Glimpses of the Great*, 1930.

24. From an August 7, 1941, letter discussing responses to his 1941 essay "Science and Religion," quoted in Max Jammer, *Einstein and Religion*, repr. ed. (Princeton: Princeton Univ. Press, 2011), 97.

25. http://pandagon.blogsome.com/2008/05/13/and-einstein-was-an-atheist/; no longer accessible, but these comments can be seen elsewhere on the web.

26. Austin Cline, "Einstein Quotes on Atheism & Freethought: Was Einstein an Atheist, Freethinker?" About.com, http://atheism.about.com/od/einsteingodreligion/tp/Was-Einstein-an-Atheist-.htm; accessed October 22, 2013.

27. Einstein, in a letter to Beatrice F. in response to a question about whether he was a "free thinker," December 17, 1952, quoted in *Famous Quotes from 100 Great People*.

28. http://www.celebatheists.com/wiki/Albert_Einstein.

29. http://www.positiveatheism.org/hist/quotes/einstein.htm.

30. http://www.atheistempire.com/greatminds/quotes.php?author=9.

CHAPTER 4: WHY DID EINSTEIN EMBRACE SPINOZA'S GOD?

1. Albert Einstein, *Out of My Later Years: The Scientist, Philosopher, and Man Portrayed Through His Own Words* (1950; repr., New York: Open Road, 2011), 9.

2. Einstein, "Autobiographical Notes," in *Albert Einstein: Philosopher-Scientist*, ed. and trans. Paul A. Schilpp, 3rd ed. (Peru, IL: Open Court, 1998), 3.

3. Brian Denis, *Einstein: A Life* (New York: John Wiley & Sons, 1996), 127.

4. Walter Isaacson, *Einstein: His Life and Universe*, repr. ed. (New York: Simon & Schuster, 2008).

5. Einstein, "Zu Spinozas Ethik" (poem about Spinoza written in 1920), in Max Jammer, *Einstein and Religion: Physics and Theology*, repr. ed. (Princeton, Princeton University Press, 2002), 43.

6. Max Jammer, *Einstein and Religion* (Princeton: Princeton University Press, 1999), 138–39.

7. Baruch, or Benedict, de Spinoza (November 24, 1632–February

21, 1677) was a Dutch philosopher of Portuguese Jewish origin.

8. Ronald W. Clark, *Einstein: The Life and Times*, repr. (New York: HarperCollins, 1984), 502.

9. Max Jammer, *Einstein and Religion*, repr. ed. (Princeton: Princeton Univ. Press, 2011).

10. Albert Einstein, "Religion and Science," http://www.stephen-jaygould.org/ctrl/einstein_religion.html#see, excerpted from Einstein, *The World as I See It* (Secaucus, NJ: Citadel, 1999), 24–29.

11. Ibid.

12. Isaacson, *Einstein*, 15, 2.

13. H. G. Kessler, *The Diary of a Cosmopolitan* (London: Weidenfeld and Nicolson, 1971), 157; quoted in Jammer, *Einstein and Religion* (1999), 39–40.

14. Albert Einstein, letter, 1954, quoted in Paul Blanshard, *American Freedom and Catholic Power* (n.p.: Greenwood, 1984), 10.

15. Albert Einstein, letter to Sigmund Freud, July 30, 1932, published in 1933 in Albert Einstein and Sigmund Freud, *Why War?* (n.p.: International Institute of Intellectual Cooperation, 1933).

16. Einstein, *The World as I See It*, repr. (San Diego: The Book Tree, 2007), 25.

17. Ibid.

18. Isaacson, *Einstein*, 387.

19. Einstein, *The World as I See It*, 25.

20. A. Pais, *Einstein Lived Here* (New York: Oxford Univ. Press, 1994), 118.

21. Einstein, quoted in Larry Chang, comp. and ed., *Wisdom for the Soul: Five Millennia of Prescriptions for Spiritual Healing* (Washington, DC: Gnosophia, 2006), 583.

22. Jim Green, ed., *Albert Einstein: Rebel Lives* (Melbourne: Ocean Press, 2003), 27, quoting Einstein, "The World as I See It"; emphasis added.

23. Ibid.

24. Helen Dukas and Banesh Hoffman, eds., *Albert Einstein, The Human Side: Glimpses from His Archives*, paperback ed. (Princeton: Princeton Univ. Press, 2013), 39.

25. *Science, Philosophy and Religion, A Symposium*, published by the Conference on Science, Philosophy and Religion in Their Relation to the Democratic Way of Life, Inc. (New York, 1941); later published in *Out of My Later Years* (1950; repr. 2011).

26. Einstein, *Out of My Later Years* (1950; repr., 2011), 27.

27. Anonymous, "Mileva Einstein-Maric," http://itis.volta.alessandria.it/episteme/ep4/ep4maric.htm, accessed October 31, 2013.

28. Ibid.

29. Alok Jha, "Letters reveal relative truth of Einstein's family life," *The Guardian,* July 10, 2006, http://www.theguardian.com/science/2006/jul/11/internationalnews.

30. By Hans C. Ohanian, New York: W. W. Norton, 2008.

31. Nanore Barsoumian, "Book Review: Ohanian's 'Einstein's Mistakes,'" *Armenian Weekly,* March 8, 2010, http://www.armenianweekly.com/2010/03/08/book-review-ohanian-einsteins-mistakes/.

CHAPTER 5: EINSTEIN'S "FAITH IN GOD IS CHILDLIKE"

1. Einstein, letter to philosopher Eric Gutkind, January 3, 1954, quoted in James Randerson, "Childish Superstition: Einstein's Letter Makes View of Religion Relatively Clear: Scientist's Reply to Sell for up to £8,000, and Stoke Debate over His Beliefs," *Guardian* (UK), May 12, 2008, http://www.theguardian.com/science/2008/may/12/peopleinscience.religion.

CHAPTER 6: THE BOLD ASSERTION

1. As quoted in Peter A. Bucky and Allen G. Weakland, *The Private Albert Einstein* (n.p.: Andrews & McMeel, 1992), 86.

2. Alice Calaprice, *The Expanded Quotable Einstein* (Princeton: Princeton University, 2000), 61.

3. Ibid., 63.

4. Homer Baxter Sprague, *Masterpieces in English Literature, and Lessons in the English Language, . . .* , vol. 1 (New York: J. W. Schermerhorn & Co., 1874), 89.

5. Albert Einstein, letter to an atheist (1954), in Helen Dukas and Banesh Hoffman, eds., *Albert Einstein, The Human Side: Glimpses from His Archives,* paperback ed. (Princeton: Princeton Univ. Press, 2013).

6. Albert Einstein, "Religion and Science," republished in Einstein, *The World as I See It* (Secaucus, NJ: The Citadel Press, 1999), 24–29.

7. Albert Einstein, "Religion and Science," *New York Times Magazine*, November 9, 1930, http://www.sacred-texts.com/aor/einstein/einsci.htm.

8. Albert Einstein to Guy H. Raner Jr., September 28, 1949, quoted by Michael R. Gilmore in "Just What Did Einstein Believe about God?" *Skeptic* 5, no. 2 (1997).

9. From an interview with William Hermanns in the summer of 1954, quoted in Max Jammer, *Einstein and Religion*, repr. ed. (Princeton: Princeton Univ. Press, 2011); emphasis added.

10. Albert Einstein, in James A. Haught, *2000 Years of Disbelief: Famous People with the Courage to Doubt* (Amherst, NY: Prometheus, 1996), 240.

11. Einstein, letter to philosopher Eric Gutkind, January 3, 1954, quoted in James Randerson, "Childish Superstition: Einstein's Letter Makes View of Religion Relatively Clear: Scientist's Reply to Sell for up to £8,000, and Stoke Debate over His Beliefs," *Guardian* (UK), May 12, 2008, http://www.theguardian.com/science/2008/may/12/peopleinscience.religion.

12. From Albert Einstein, *Cosmic religion: With Other Opinions and Aphorisms* (1931), quoted in Calaprice, *The Expanded Quotable Einstein*, 2nd ed., 208.

CHAPTER 7: WHY EINSTEIN WAS NOT AN ATHEIST

1. Albert Einstein, letter to Maurice Solovine, January 1, 1951, in Albert Einstein, *Letters to Solovine: 1906–1955* (New York: Open Road Media, 2011).

2. Walter Isaacson, "Einstein & Faith," *Time* magazine, April 5, 2007, http://content.time.com/time/magazine/article/0,9171,1607298-2,00.html.

3. From a 1930 interview with J. Murphy and J. W. N. Sullivan, quoted in Douglas Kenneth Peary, *Humanist Heroes* (n.p.: Xlibris, 2003).

4. Albert Einstein to Guy H. Raner Jr., September 28, 1949, quoted by Michael R. Gilmore in "Just What Did Einstein Believe about God?" *Skeptic* 5, no. 2 (1997).

5. Alice Calaprice, *The Expanded Quotable Einstein* (Princeton: Princeton University, 2000), 214.

6. Richard Dawkins, *The Ancestor's Tale: A Pilgrimage to the Dawn of Evolution,* repr. (New York: Houghton Mifflin Harcourt, 2005), 613.

7. Chris Nitardy, *Stumbling Blocks of Evolution: Post Darwin Evidence Points to a Creator* (n.p.: Xulon, 2012), 215.

8. Karen Matthews, "Curious About Astronomy? Ask an Astronomer," Cornell University, October 2002, http://curious.astro.cornell.edu/question.php?number=364.

9. Alison Snyder, posted August 21, 2006, in response to a question from Michael Y.: "What Existed before the Big Bang?" scienceline, http://scienceline.org/2006/08/ask-snyder-bang/.

10. Nitardy, *Stumbling Blocks of Evolution,* 216.

11. Victor J. Stenger, "A Scenario for a Natural Origin of Our Universe Using a Mathematical Model Based on Established Physics and Cosmology," http://www.qcc.cuny.edu/socialSciences/ppecorino/INTRO_TEXT/Chapter%203%20Religion/CH-3-Documents/ch3-Stengler-on-Origin-math-model.pdf, 3, 12.

12. Mark I. Vuletic, "Creation ex Nihilo," *Observer,* 1997, https://groups.google.com/forum/#!topic/atheism-vs-christianity/OVvbyFrStNs.

13. Brad Lemley, "Guth's Grand Guess," *Discover* magazine, April 2002, 36, http://discovermagazine.com/2002/apr/cover#.UnKZH3DUBNs.

CHAPTER 8: EINSTEIN'S "RELIGION"

1. As quoted in George Thomas White Patrick and Frank Miller Chapman, *Introduction to Philosophy,* rev. ed. (New York: Houghton Mifflin, 1935), 44.

2. Albert Einstein, response to atheist Alfred Kerr, 1927, in H. G. Kessler, *The Diary of a Cosmopolitan* (London: Weidenfeld and Nicolson, 1971), 157; quoted in Max Jammer, *Einstein and Religion* (1999), 39–40.

3. Letter to philosopher Eric Gutkind, January 3, 1954, quoted in *Famous Quotes from 100 Great People* (MobileReference, 2011).

4. Albert Einstein, "Religion and Science," *New York Times Magazine*, November 9, 1930.

CHAPTER 9: ANSWERING
EINSTEIN'S DIFFICULTIES

1. "Mein Weltbild" (1931) (i.e., *My World-view*, or *My View of the World* or *The World as I See It* (as translated for the title essay of the 1949 book: "The World as I See It"). Various translated editions have been published of this essay; or portions of it, including one titled "What I Believe"; another compilation which includes it is *Ideas and Opinions* (1954).

2. Jim Green, ed., *Albert Einstein: Rebel Lives* (Melbourne: Ocean Press, 2003), 27, quoting Einstein, "The World as I See It."

3. Albert Einstein, *Autobiographical Notes*, Paul Arthur Schilpp, ed. (Peru, IL: Open Court, 1991).

4. Einstein, quoted in *Does God Exist? The Craig-Flew Debate*, Stan Wallace, ed. (Hants, UK/Burlington, VT: Ashgate, 2003), 191.

5. *Science, Philosophy and Religion, A Symposium*, published by the Conference on Science, Philosophy and Religion in Their Relation to the Democratic Way of Life, Inc. (New York, 1941); later published in Albert Einstein, *Out of My Later Years* (1950; repr., New York: Open Road, 2011).

6. Einstein, *Out of My Later Years: The Scientist, Philosopher, and Man Portrayed Through His Own Words*, chap. 8, "Science and Religion."

7. Ibid.

8. Albert Einstein, "Religion and Science: Irreconcilable?" a response to a greeting sent by the Liberal Ministers' Club of New York City, published in *The Christian Register*, June, 1948; and later published in *Ideas and Opinions* (New York: Crown, 1954), http://www.sacred-texts.com/aor/einstein/einsci.htm.

9. See Marc Horne, "Richard Dawkins Calls for Arrest of Pope Benedict XVI," *Times Online*, April 10, 2010, on the website of the Richard Dawkins Foundation for Reason and Science, http://old.richarddawkins.net/articles/5415.

10. Richard Dawkins, "Ratzinger Is the Perfect Pope," *Washington Post*, March 27, 2010, posted on the website of the Richard Dawkins Foundation for Reason and Science, http://old.richard-dawkins.net/articles/5341.

11. Richard Dawkins said that life "could come about in the following way: it could be that uh, at some earlier time somewhere in the universe a civilization e-evolved . . . by probably by some kind of Darwinian means to a very, very high level of technology and designed a form of life that they seeded onto . . . perhaps this . . . this planet . . . *and that designer could well be a higher intelligence from elsewhere in the universe." Expelled;* emphasis added. See http://www.getbig.com/boards/index.php?topic=210565.45;imode.

12. "Don't Talk to Aliens, Warns Stephen Hawking," *Sunday Times* (UK), April 25, 2010, posted on the Fox News website, at http://www.foxnews.com/scitech/2010/04/25/dont-talk-aliens-warns-stephen-hawking/.

CHAPTER 10: ALBERT EINSTEIN AND THE ATOMIC BOMB

1. Einstein, in *The Saturday Evening Post*, October 26, 1929.

2. Piero Scaruffi, "Wars and Casualties of the 20th and 21st Centuries," http://www.scaruffi.com/politics/massacre.html.

3. Ronald Clark, *Einstein: The Life and Times* (n.p.: Hodder & Stoughton, 1973), 428.

4. *Wikipedia*, s.v. "Einstein–Szilárd letter," accessed November 6, 2013, http://en.wikipedia.org/wiki/Einstein%E2%80%93Szil%C3%A1rd_letter.

5. Weart and Szilard, 125; Clark, *Einstein: The Life and Times*, 680.

6. Richard Rhodes, *The Making of the Atomic Bomb* (New York: Simon and Schuster, 2012), 377.

7. Doug Long, "Albert Einstein and the Atomic Bomb, http://www.doug-long.com/einstein.htm; accessed November 6, 2013.

8.   Ibid.

9.   "Einstein Deplores Use of Atom Bomb," *New York Times*, August 19, 1946, 1.

10.   Albert Einstein, *Einstein on Peace*, Otto Nathan and Heinz Norden, eds., Avenel 1981 ed. (Random House Value Publishing, 1988), 589.

11.   Clark, *Einstein: The Life and Times*, 752.

CHAPTER 11: SCIENCE FORUMS

1.   *Science, Philosophy and Religion, A Symposium*, published by the Conference on Science, Philosophy and Religion in Their Relation to the Democratic Way of Life, Inc. (New York, 1941); later published in *Out of My Later Years* (1950; repr. 2011).

2.   Adapted from "Interview: Ray Comfort Answers Your Questions," posted April 8, 2010, by "Cap'n Refsmmat" on scienceforums.net, http://www.scienceforums.net/topic/47512-interview-ray-comfort-answers-your-questions/.

3.   See www.OriginIntoSchools.com.

4.   Richard Dawkins, *The Ancestor's Tale: A Pilgrimage to the Dawn of Evolution* (New York: Houghton Mifflin, 2004), 613; emphasis added.

5.   See http://www.wnd.com/2010/03/127345/; http://www.wnd.com/2010/10/212249/ .

6.   Theodosius Dobzhansky, "Nothing in Biology Makes Sense Except in the Light of Evolution" (essay), 1973, http://people.delphiforums.com/lordorman/Dobzhansky.pdf; http://www.pbs.org/wgbh/evolution/library/10/2/text_pop/l_102_01.html.

7.   It is popular for atheists to refer to the Bible cynically as a "Bronze-age" book, when only Old Testament history lies in the Bronze Age, and *that* only in the latest part of the Bronze Age, as well as the early Iron Age.

CHAPTER 12: SKEPTICS' DIFFICULTIES WITH GOD

1. "Mein Weltbild" (1931) (i.e., *My World-view*, or *My View of the World* or *The World as I See It* (as translated for the title essay of the 1949 book: "The World as I See It"). Various translated editions have been published of this essay; or portions of it, including one titled "What I Believe"; another compilation which includes it is *Ideas and Opinions* (1954).

2. These are atheists who have written to me on my blog. Thousands of readers write to me on my Facebook page (I have had to ban over 3,000 atheists/skeptics for bad language this year alone).

3. See comments to note # 2 above.

4. "Agnostic." Merriam-Webster.com. Accessed November 7, 2013. http://www.merriam-webster.com/dictionary/agnostic.

5. "An Atheist's Question," posted on January 27, 2010, http://www.goodreads.com/author_blog_posts/293079-an-atheist-s-question.

6. A question posed in "Was Hitler a Christian?" posted on website of *Worldview Times*, January 26, 2010, http://worldviewweekend.com/worldview-times/article.php?articleid=5780. The response that follows is adapted from my response in that article.

7. This question, too, was published in "Was Hitler a Christian?" My response here is from that article.

8. This question and the response that follow are also from Comfort, "Thinking about Lust."

9. Quoted from Ray Comfort, "Interesting Comment from an Atheist," posted December 31, 2009, http://old.worldviewweekend.com/worldview-times/print.php?&ArticleID=5709.

10. This question and a portion of the response that follows can be seen at http://www.goodreads.com/author_blog_posts/255410-a-serious-question-about-lust, imported from my own blog and published December 19, 2009. The response has been adapted for this book.

11. Ray Comfort, *The Defender's Guide for Life's Toughest Questions* (Green Forest, AR: New Leaf, 2011), 86–87.

12. Abridged from ibid., 140–42.

13. Ibid., 41.

14. Ibid., 40. Portions of my response, which follows, can be seen at http://www.goodreads.com/author_blog_posts/208418-another-so-ray-you-don-t-know-the-answer-question.

15. Ray Comfort, "Big Words from Little Woody," posted October 19, 2009, http://www.worldviewweekend.com:81/worldview-times/print.php?&ArticleID=5501.

CHAPTER 13: SKEPTICS'
DIFFICULTIES WITH THE BIBLE

1. Albert Einstein, "Principles of Research" public address given in Berlin, Physical Society, for Max Planck's sixtieth birthday, 1918.

2. "A Response from Ray Comfort," Uniting the Body of Christ, March 5, 2010, http://unitingthebodyofchrist.blogspot.com/2010/03/response-from-ray-comfort.html.

3. Charles Spurgeon, "Hideous Discovery," sermon no. 1911, Metropolitan Tabernacle Pulpit 1, Volume 32 www.spurgeongems.org.

4. See www.evolutionvsGod.com.

CHAPTER 14: THE SEVEN MOST
IMPORTANT QUESTIONS

1. Albert Einstein, Out of My Later Years: The Scientist, Philosopher, and Man Portrayed Through His Own Words (1950; repr., New York: Open Road, 2011).

2. Einstein, "Everything Is a Miracle," Awakin (blog), posted November 18, 2002, http://www.awakin.org/read/view.php?tid=255.

3. Dictionary.com, s.v. "covet," http://dictionary.reference.com/browse/covet.

4. Free Dictionary, s.v. "adultery," http://legal-dictionary.thefree-dictionary.com/adultery.

5. Specialized parts of the military allow this.

6. Stephen Fitzpatrick, *The Australian*, quoted in "Beheaded Girls Were Ramadan 'Trophies,'" Jihad Watch, posted by Robert on November 9, 2006, http://www.jihadwatch.org/cgi-sys/cgi-wrap/br0nc0s/managed-mt/mt-srch.cgi?search=indonesia%20&IncludeBlogs=1&limit=20&page=54.

7. "How Can You Be Sure if You Are a True Christian?" baby center community, posted on February 17, 2010, quoting Ray Comfort, *Atheist Central* (blog), February 16, 2010, http://community.babycenter.com/post/a21665661/how_can_you_be_sure_if_you_are_a_true_christian.

8. Ibid.

CHAPTER 15: EINSTEIN'S POPULAR IDOL

1. Albert Einstein, in a letter to M. Berkowitz, October 25, 1950; Einstein Archive 59-215; from Alice Calaprice, *The Expanded Quotable Einstein* (Princeton: Princeton University, 2000), 216.

2. Bible History Online, *Fausset's Bible Dictionary*, s.v. "idol," http://www.bible-history.com/faussets/I/Idol/.

3. Mark Twain, in a letter to Olivia Clemens, July 17, 1889.

4. *Mark Twain's Notebook*, as quoted at http://www.twainquotes.com/God.html.

5. *Mark Twain, a Biography*, at ibid.

6. See, for example, http://www.classicreader.com/book/1930/9/.

7. See http://www.twainquotes.com/Sex.html.

8. Antony Flew, with Roy Abraham Varghese, *There Is a God: How the World's Most Notorious Atheist Changed His Mind* (New York: HarperCollins, 2009), 9.

9. Ibid., 15.

10. Ibid., 89.

11. William Grimes, "Antony Flew, Philosopher and Ex-Atheist, Dies at 87," *International New York Times*, April 16, 2010, http://www.nytimes.com/2010/04/17/arts/17flew.html.

12. *The Freethinker* 90 (1970): 147.

13. This question can be seen on Good Reads, at http://www.goodreads.com/author_blog_posts/424524-the-ex-christian-atheist, posted May 7, 2010.

CHAPTER 16: WHY I TRUST GOD

1. Albert Einstein, quoted in Edward Howe Cotton, *Has Science Discovered God? A Symposium of Modern Scientific Opinion* (1931), 101.
2. See http://www.youtube.com/watch?v=Tvitmq7KkPE.

CHAPTER 17: THE FEAR OF DYING: EINSTEIN'S LAST WORDS

1. Helen Dukas, *Albert Einstein, The Human Side* (Princeton: Princeton Univ. Press, 1981), 43.
2. J. R. Cohen and L. M. Graver, "The Ruptured Abdominal Aortic Aneurysm of Albert Einstein," *Surgery, Gynecology & Obstetrics* 170, no. 5: (May 1990), 455–58.
3. Walter Isaacson, "Einstein & Faith," *Time*, April 5, 2007, http://www.time.com/time/magazine/article/0,9171,1607298-2,00.html.
4. *Saturday Evening Post*, October 26, 1929, 17.
5. Alice Calaprice, *The Expanded Quotable Einstein* (Princeton: Princeton University, 2000), 61.
6. Einstein, quoted in Paul Arthur Schilpp, *Albert Einstein: Philosopher-Scientist*, 3rd ed. (n.p.: Open Court, 1998).
7. Diana Kormos Buchwald et al., eds., *The Collected Papers of Albert Einstein*, vol. 10: *The Berlin Years* (English translation of selected texts) (Princeton University Press, 2006), http://press.princeton.edu/chapters/s8332.pdf, 11.
8. Isaacson, "Einstein & Faith."

Index